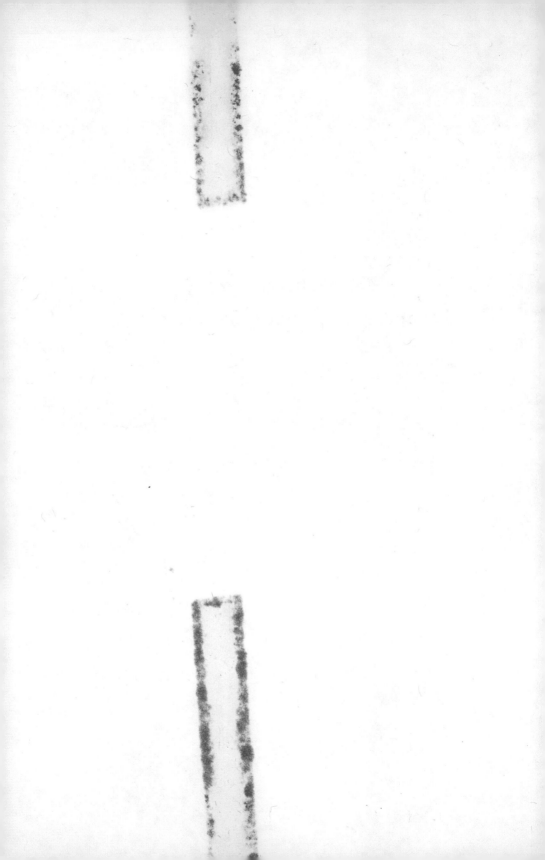

Illustrated Handbook
of Band Formations:

200 Models with
Recommended Music Selections

Carrol M. Butts

Parker Publishing Co., Inc.   West Nyack, New York

ALSO BY THE AUTHOR

*How to Arrange and Rehearse
Football Band Shows*

© 1975 *by*

PARKER PUBLISHING COMPANY, INC.

West Nyack, N.Y.

Library of Congress Cataloging in Publication Data

Butts, Carrol M
    Illustrated handbook of band formations.

    1. Marching bands. I. Title.
MT733.4.B89   785'.06'7108   74-34030
ISBN 0-13-451245-6

Printed in the United States of America

How to Benefit from This Ready Reference

This book is an extensive creation of original field formations, with 200 varieties accompanied by over 1,000 song titles that are known to the general public.

The most common problem confronting all marching band directors is simple but critical: creation of new and interesting shows, and projection of this to the audience. Most directors are quite inventive, through training, experience, and necessity. At the same time, they are constantly in the throes of marching band season with its many problems.

Some of these formations have been ideated and used by directors prior to this publication; however, the shapes and scale proportions are unlike any others available.

Each formation, with its related music titles, is strong enough to stand alone, which is a definite advantage when the director needs just one single idea or formation. Should the director's requirement exceed a single topic, the theme index, containing 49 complete shows and hundreds of song titles, may well supply the total answer.

The work, therefore, is intended to be a comprehensive source of ideas, formations, and music.

Limited time is another problem connected with the production of shows. Even when an idea has already been formed, the succeeding steps are time-consuming. In order to ease this situation, the book was created in the form shown, which includes these time-saving features:

1. All formations are in exact scale proportions; no reworking is required.

2. The field charts are in exact scale proportion.

3. The formations show exactly where every band member is placed.

4. The block band key shows all members by rank and file letter and number.

5. The illustrations are clear enough to be photo-copied and distributed directly to each band member.

6. The song titles are also printed on each formation, and if the director decides to use this music, the student already has this information. If the director decides to use other music, he certainly has that option, and may simply write in other song titles before photo-copying is done.

In the following pages, there is much discussion concerning these areas, related problems, and remedies to many of the troublesome phases connected with show production. The discussion includes:

1. field check points.

2. formation size and possible alteration.

3. proportion connected to the low bleacher situation.

4. band size other than the 60 as prescribed, in reference to the formations.

5. individual spacing intervals.

6. three types of movement used between formations.

7. time limit considerations.

8. theme development and examples.

9. sound factors—problems and solutions.

10. rehearsal procedures.

11. props and scripts.

Further reading will indicate the full purpose of the book, which is to help ideate, choose music for, rehearse effectively, and project strong shows in a consistent manner to the public.

Formation Size and Proportion

All formations are designed for a 60-member band. The majority of drawings are spaced from the upper third insert down to the near sideline, in height. In width, most designs are within the two 35-yard lines.

It is possible to magnify any formation by altering the height or length to satisfy placement of more band members. Another option, when considering extra members, suggests closer positioning of members. Neither variation will inhibit the general shape of any formation, unless drastic changes are made.

In general, it would be inadvisable to reduce the size of any formation, since all are designed for use with the average bleacher situation. Any formation that is reduced in size to any extent will lose clarity and simplicity. Enlargement enhances clarity, but at the same time, invites precision problems because of the distance and time-lag. Vertical enlargement should be used when the bleachers are quite low. Expansion from left to right would serve no practical purpose, in any case.

For an example of expansion, (to be used with low bleachers) let us use the Badge formation on page 6. From ground zero or from there to 20 or 30 feet above, the formation will appear wide but not very tall. Expansion in height is needed. Ranks A, B, G, H, and I require no alteration from left to right. Some vertical extension within these ranks would enhance the specific segments of the formation. For example, rank A members 1 and 7 are stationed (vertically) 9 steps apart. By increasing the number of steps to 13 or 14, with inside members repositioning themselves proportionately, the height would be greater than shown. Rank members in G, H, and I are only 2½ steps apart from top to bottom. If these distances were enlarged to 4 steps, we have further heightening in this portion of the formation. Vertical members, which are mostly in ranks C, D, E, and F, are placed 3 steps apart. If this number of steps were increased to 4 or 5, then the total formation would be heightened considerably, and would offer greater clarity to the bleacher audience. The top extremity of the badge would be approximately 14 steps higher, about midway between the upper third insert and the top sideline. The result, on paper, reflects a taller image, but from low-level viewing, the formation will appear in excellent proportion.

Variations in band size can be adapted to these formations in several ways. If a unit has fewer than 60 members, twirlers, flag-bearers, or rifle-bearers may be inserted into the formation, or individual spacing may be enlarged, without changing the size of the diagram. If a band has more than the prescribed 60 members, individual spacing may be diminished, therefore providing room to insert more members. Sometimes a rank, such as the percussion unit, may be stationed somewhat removed from the total unit. It is a rather common practice to place the percussion section in a separate situation, which enhances the sound, and, if carefully done, the formation will not be weakened. One other alternative would be to add something to the design, such as a circle within the badge, in this case. It is advisable to have a few extra band members available in case of sickness. It is not difficult to substitute members in picture formations, opposed to substitution in precision-drill work.

In most instances, members are equidistant from one to another, with exceptions as shown in specific formations.

Individual Movements

Individual movements from one formation to another may be divided into three categories, each of which have certain advantages over the others.

1. scatter movement

This type is the least attractive of the three, but it does offer the quickest method of reaching positions in the next formation. Each member takes the shortest route, disregarding all other member movements, except to avoid collision. The scatter movement can be done in cadence, or without measured tempo. Occasionally, members can run into the new position. This, again, is not visually attractive, but if time is short, the technique has some merit.

2. rank movement by single-file

This type of movement is much more appealing, and

it fits the formations as they are set up. Each rank is shown by letter and number in every formation, which automatically suggests rank movement from one diagram to another. Single-file simply means following the leader, which can be #1 or #7 in each rank. Whichever rank extremity member (1 or 7) happens to be nearest, the next position automatically becomes rank leader for that specific movement. Rarely would #1 or #7 always be the leader in an entire series of formations. Single-file rank movement should be done in cadence.

3. rank movement by flank

There are certain instances when a flanking situation is most applicable, and when it is, the rank marches intact, side-by-side, to the new position. There are also cases that might suggest both types of rank movement, one after the other. For example, a rank might proceed in single-file to a certain point, execute a flanking movement, and continue to march into position in side-by-side rank formation. As in #2, movement to a cadence is preferable.

Numbers 2 and 3 are definitely recommended as being the most attractive, but both styles take more time than number 1. It follows that when moving in any of the three styles, in tempo, playing may be done while marching.

Development of Show Themes

In addition to the 200 formations in this book, there is a theme index, suggesting 49 different shows. Each show offers several related formations, and each formation has several suggested song titles.

1. time limits

An average show might include five to eight formations, with dependence solely upon time limits. There are two phases with the term "time limit." The most obvious phase is the overall amount of time accorded the band on field for the half-time performance. This block of time must be used in connection with the secondary time limit, which is concerned with the amount of time used in each formation. For example, if the band uses a complete musical arrangement that lasts two or three minutes, obviously, the number of formations cannot exceed three or four. However, if the band plays sections of music (or without repeats), the number of formations could be expanded to nearly double the figure just mentioned. The number of formations used by the director may vary from show to show, with dependence upon at least two factors:

    a. amount of rehearsal time available

    b. difficulty of formations and music

With the time element in mind, we can proceed to the next phase.

2. theme development

Although there are numerous themes shown in the index, this certainly does not preclude the possibility of creating additional topics with appropriate music.

We might, then, examine themes and development, by showing the various tangents that may spring from a single thought.

Presented here are several examples that indicate ideas and subsequent growth or treatment into a full half-time performance:

Example 1

    A. first idea: "tribute to composers or music"

    B. composer's names: Beethoven, Gershwin, Ravel, Rossini

    C. music titles: "Moonlight Sonata," "Rhapsody in Blue," "Bolero," "Barber of Seville"

    D. formations: Moon, Piano, Spanish Fan, Straight Razor

This first idea shows how one thought may lead to many others in logical sequence. The tangents may appear in the form of music, formations, or action, in turn based upon places, things, or objects.

Example 2

   A. first idea: "birds"

   B. music titles: "Flamingo," "Red Wing," "Under the Double Eagle," "Sparrow in the Tree Top," "Bye Bye Blackbird"

   C. formations: Flamingo or Crane, Blackbird, Eagle Symbol, Birdcage, Tree, Gulls

Example 3

   A. first idea: "news"

   B. music titles: N in "news" suggests "North to Alaska"

                    E in "news" suggests "East of the Sun and West of the Moon"

                    W in "news" suggests "How the West Was Won"

                    S in "news" suggests "South"

                    (news comes from the four directions)

   C. formations: Igloo, Sun or Compass, Rifle or Horse, Confederate Cape

Second Opinion

   B_1. news-topics: crime, rodeo, war, holiday

   C_1. formations: Badge, Horse, Cannon, Beach Umbrella

   D. music titles: "Peter Gunn," "Home on the Range," "Battle Hymn of the Republic," "Holiday for Strings"

Example 4

   A. first idea: "dance forms"

   B. dance types: minuet, waltz, square dance, jitterbug, twist

   C. formation: Dance Hall or Stage

   D. action: several members doing the minuet, waltz, or other dances.

E. music titles: Minuet in G, "Blue Danube," "Turkey in the Straw," "Little Brown Jug," "The Twist"

Almost any word, current event, action, place, or situation can be expanded to a complete show of at least four segments, by employing word-association. In turn, the four segments suggest appropriate music.

A few examples of word-association in theme ideas and development include:

love—marriage, heart, arrow, cross, church, ring
politics—donkey, elephant, Capitol building, dollar sign, campaigning (travel modes), speech, T.V., radio
growing up—pre-teenage, teenage, marriage or college age, middle age, old age
science—biology, medicine, space travel, mathematics, chemistry, zoology
emotion—love, hate, happiness, sadness, excitement, etc.

The possibilities are unlimited.

Sound Factors

The block band key shown in this book features the brasses in a forward position, backed up by the percussion section. This presents a powerful, if somewhat brass-oriented, sound. Even so, when the formations are used, the various woodwinds will be heard. Some directors favor this instrumentation placement, while others prefer woodwinds in the forward position, which gives a better concert sound. In either case, once the ranks are designated by instrument, the formations are formed as shown.

In either set-up, there is no problem of adequate sound with a mature or large band. However, in the young or small band, there will be a basic problem of weak sound.

There are several solutions available to help offset this problem. These solutions have no relationship to the formations themselves, as they should remain unchanged.

To strengthen the sound, and thus enhance any formation, these suggestions are given:

1. use easy music in comfortable band keys

2. do not march and play at the same time, if the band has a loss of sound when doing so

3. if the formation requires movement, use woodwinds in the moving segments, so that the brasses and percussion can remain in static positions and project a stronger sound

4. arrange music to fit one's band, using simple scoring, doublings, unisons, strong rhythms, etc.

5. keep brasses together, and percussion close by—other instruments may be spaced with less chance of precision problems

6. conduct any selection that presents difficulty in precision

7. place all formations as close to the audience as possible, by positioning the bottom members of any diagram on the nearest sideline

8. use fewer selections but observe repeats

Rehearsal Procedures

In order to project the formations in this book to full advantage of the audience, there are several rehearsal techniques available than can help insure this. This is no substitute for drill time on the field, in most instances, but some of the following movements can be done inside or outside. They are basic movements as follows:

1. at ease
2. attention
3. forward march
4. mark time
5. halt
6. right and left face
7. right and left flank
8. rear-march (while marching and from attention)
9. right and left obliques
10. 8 steps to 5 yards

After these fundamentals are secure, the formations will evolve quickly, with proper intervals and correct procedures to the individual's placement. Once the rank concept is understood and practiced, the entire idea of creating the formations will be clarified, since the transformation from one to any other formation will be similar. Naturally, the director will have to chart each rank's direction of progress when changing formations. However, since this is done by ranks, it is not difficult to plot, nor does it involve very much time. A rank (on paper) can simply be circled. Then an arrow can be attached to the circle, showing the new direction leading to the next formation. The director must also advise rank members as to which type of movement is to be made. The last two types can be used at the same time, but it would be inconsistent to use either of these two with the scatter system.

It is suggested that all of these formations be rehearsed in the same sequence each time a new one is introduced. From any given point (whether it is a company front, several fronts, block band, or previous formation) the band should walk into the new formation. Once in the approximate positions, the members should line up with the several checkpoints that are on the field. These include all yard lines, sidelines, upper and lower third inserts, and both goalposts (which include three points-center and both front and rear posts).

Since all lines on these charts represent a regular step of 22½ inches, the number of steps may also be counted. After walking into the new formation from the previous one perhaps two times, then the movement may take place in cadence, with drum accompaniment. In one rehearsal, the band should be able to walk into five or six new formations. After each formation is reached, however, the director must examine and make corrections as needed, particularly the first time the diagram is formed.

In every formation there will be "key" members that all others look to for their own placement. The key members must be extremely reliable and accurate. They will be the members who are on certain extremities, specific yard lines, actual points, etc. Sometimes, too, these members will be in the center of the formation.

In long files that are either horizontal or in a diagonal position, it is advisable to have the end members establish their positions first and raise one arm for the inside members to guide on. The raised arm procedure may be dropped as soon as all file members can line up correctly without it. Also, in the long file formations, members should guide right and left, to both ends, instead of guiding center or front.

During the second rehearsal, all diagrams should be formed in cadence. Inside practice on the music should precede all outside practice, making it possible to start playing and marching into the formation during the second outside rehearsal.

Some directors prefer that members march all the time while on field (which is exhausting), while others would rather have the members halt when destinations are reached. Signals to start playing are usually given by whistle or drum figures. Roll-offs can be used when the music is in march tempo, but some other signal must be employed when the music is in any other tempo or signature. Some music must simply be directed. Starting whistles or drum patterns must be used following a fermata at the end of a selection, since there is no tempo indication.

Repetitious rehearsing of the techniques just mentioned will insure a smooth performance, with continuity in the visual aspect of formation-to-formation sequences.

Props and Scripts

1. props

Although props are kept to a minimum in this book, a few formations require them, which suggests that a concise discussion should be made regarding the possibilities.

Certain formations can be enhanced by using props, but if the prop situation is overdone, it has a weakening and/or distracting effect on the band performance.

When the occasion calls for props, they should be:

a. closely related to the formation (if the props have to be announced to the audience, they are inadequate and should be adapted)

   b. light but strong

   c. kept out of sight until used

   d. used in practice several times, to insure against any type of failure—human or structural

   e. large enough to convey the idea and fit the proportion of the formation

   f. uncomplicated

2. scripts

All formation shows require a related script, which must satisfy certain requirements. It should be neither too concise nor lengthy, but at the same time, should augment the show.

A good public address system is a great asset, but in many cases, the average system is mediocre. As a result, reliance upon a strong script just cannot be insured at all times. Obviously, a fine script couldn't save a bad show, nor could a bad script ruin a good show, although the latter could be the case if the script ran on and on, ruining what sound the band provides.

An adequate script should introduce the band, the director, and the drum major. Band size and nickname should also be included.

The show theme should be announced next, with music titles mentioned just before the music starts. Reading the script while the band is playing is ineffective and distracting. However, there are times when some description is desirable, such as when the band is executing some unusual work, when not playing. Most of the time, though, it is the band's responsibility to provide both audio-visual entertainment, with the script in an introductory role, with some commentary as needed.

It is recommended that a mature speaking voice be used, and that the speaker attend the last rehearsal or two, using the public address system in syncronization with the show.

Carrol M. Butts

Contents

Formation Listing

Index of Themes

Theme	Related formations and page numbers
Animals	ant 3, barn 10, barn and silo 11, camel 30, chicken or turkey 44, dinosaur 63, dog 65, horse 97, Noah's Ark 115, snake 149, snake and basket 150, tent, circus 172, turtle 185.
Armed forces	airplane 1, anchor 2, bomb 21, bugler 27, cannon 35, cap, Confederate 36, flag 79, hat, sailor 95, machine gun 108, periscope 124, rifle 136, ship 143, soldier 152, spear 155, stripes 162, submarine 163, sword 166, tank 168, tent, pup 173, tomahawk 177, victory sign 189, walkie-talkies 191.
Birds	birdbath 17, birdhouse 18, birds, gulls 19, chicken or turkey 44, leaf 104, tree, Christmas 181, tree, palm 182, tree, shade 183.
Birthday	cake 28, calendar 29, candelabra 33, candle 34.
Anniversary	face, happy 74, flower 80, glass, wine 87, heart 96, wishing well 200.
Business	booth, carnival 23, cash register 41, coffee pot 52, dollar sign 66, question mark 133, skyline 146, telephone 170, whistle 196.
City life	Arch of Triumph 4, bridge 26, car 38, dollar sign 66, Eiffel Tower 71, fountain 81, light, traffic 106, parking meter 121, sign,

Block Band Key

Please note that rank designation is by letter, while file designation is by number.

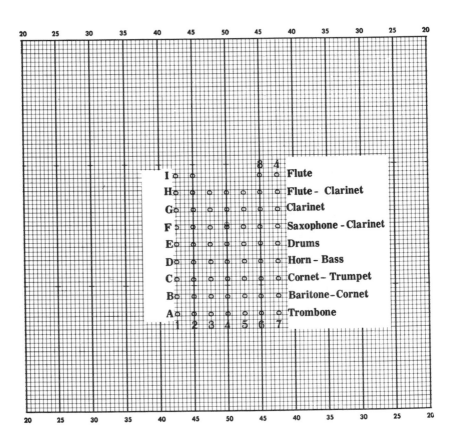

FORMATIONS

Airplane

Music: "Air Force Song," "Those Magnificent Men in Their Flying Machines," "I'm Shooting High," "The High and the Mighty."

Action: Entire formation moves to right, optional.

Props: None.

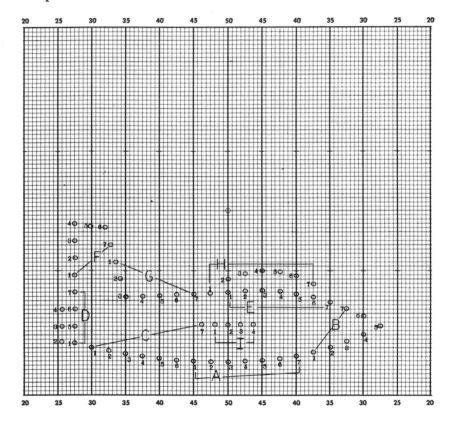

(See page xxvi for Block Band Key to Diagrams.)

1

Anchor

Music: "Anchors Aweigh," "Blow the Man Down," "By the Beautiful Sea," "Ebb Tide," "Drifting and Dreaming."

Action: None.

Props: None.

Charts by permission of Southern Music Company

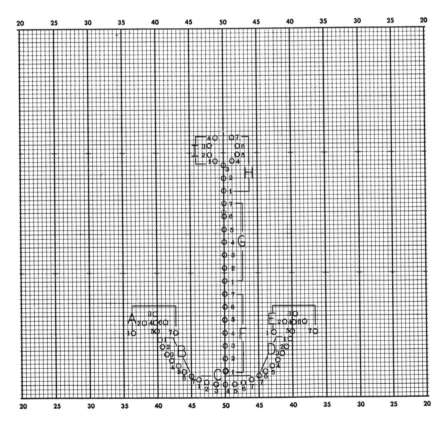

(See page xxvi for Block Band Key to Diagrams.)

Ant

Music: "Picnic," "Blueberry Hill," "The Happy Wanderer," "Dig You Later," "Climb Every Mountain," "High Society," "I've Been Working on the Railroad."

Action: Legs and feeler move, optional.

Props: None.

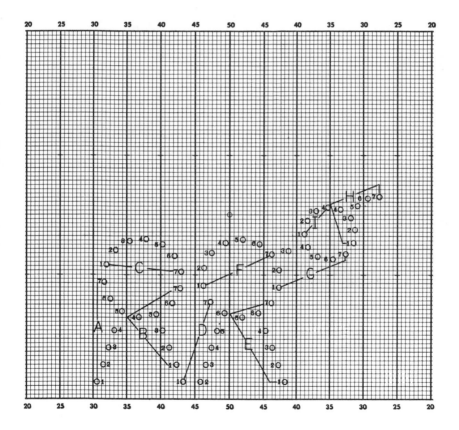

(See page xxvi for Block Band Key to Diagrams.)

3

Arch of Triumph

Music: "I Love Paris," "April in Paris," "Ballet Parisien," "American in Paris," "March from Aida," "La Marsellaise."

Action: None.

Props: None.

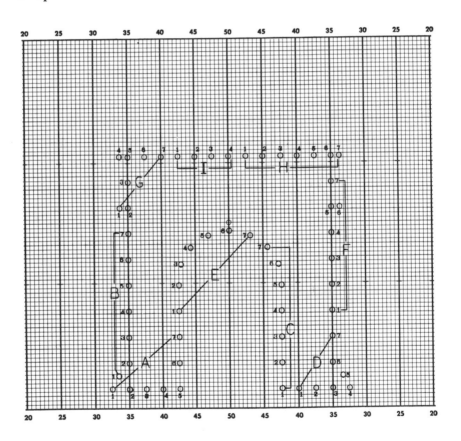

(See page xxvi for Block Band Key to Diagrams.)

Arrow

Music: "Walk Right In," "Walk, Don't Run," "Walk on By," "Where the Boys Are," "Turn! Turn! Turn!"

Action.   None.

Props: None.

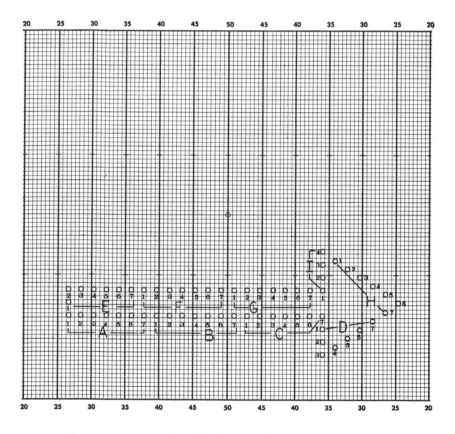

(See page xxvi for Block Band Key to Diagrams.)

5

Badge

Music: "Theme from Dragnet," "Prisoner of Love," "Hernando's Hideway," "Theme from Hawaii Five-O," "Why Don't You Believe Me?"

Action: None.

Props: None.

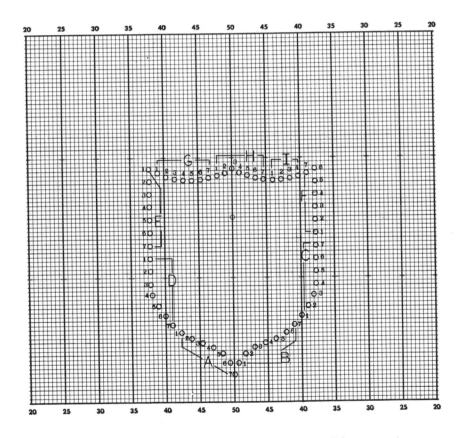

(see page xxvi for Block Band Key to Diagrams.)

Balloon

Music: "Up, Up and Away," "Around the World in 80 Days," "The High and the Mighty," "Beyond the Blue Horizon."

Action: Entire formation rises, optional.

Props: Two ropes.

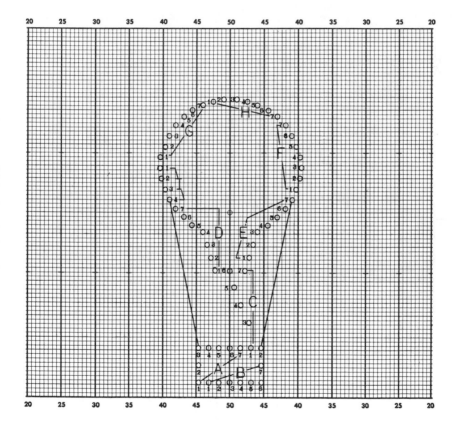

(See page xxvi for Block Band Key to Diagrams.)

Balloons, carnival

Music: "Cathy's Clown," "Meet Me in St. Louis, Louis," "The Merry-Go-Round Broke Down," "Make-Believe," "Born Free."

Action: Balloons float freely, optional.

Props: Three strings.

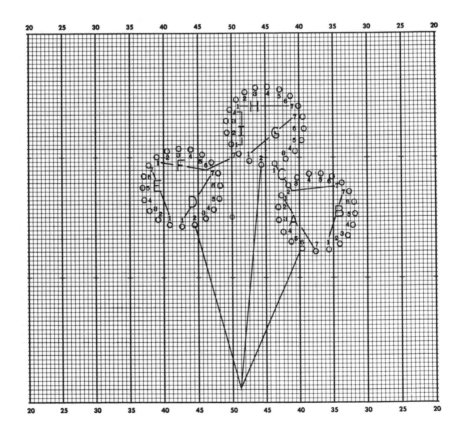

(See page xxvi for Block Band Key to Diagrams.)

Barbell

Music: "There'll Be Some Changes Made," "High Hopes," "Too Fat Polka," "Up, Up and Away," "Sugartime."

Action: Entire formation rises, optional.

Props: None.

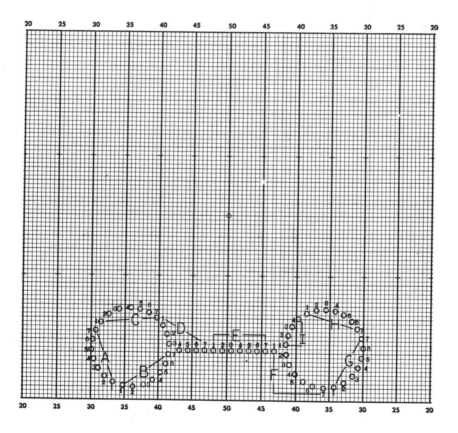

(See page xxvi for Block Band Key to Diagrams.)

9

Barn

Music: "The Farmer in the Dell," "This Is My Country," "Summertime," "The Old Grey Mare," "Oh What a Beautiful Morning."

Action: None.

Props: None.

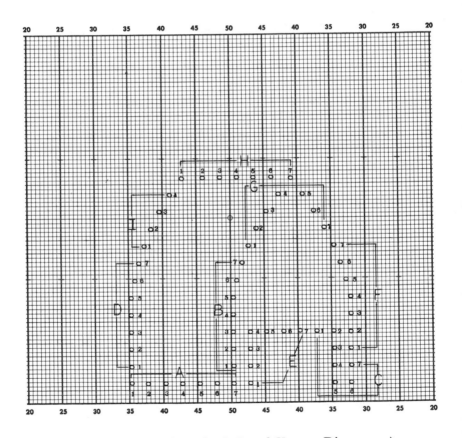

(See page xxvi for Block Band Key to Diagrams.)

10

Barn and Silo

Music·   "Old MacDonald Had a Farm," "The Farmer in the Dell," "Green Fields," "Summertime," "Green Green Grass of Home."

Action: None.

Props: None.

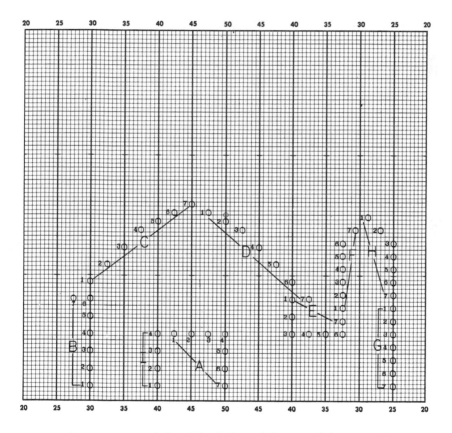

(See page xxvi for Block Band Key to Diagrams.)

Barometer

Music: "Windy," "Sunny," "Blue Skies," "Stormy Weather,"
          "Rain-Drops Keep Falling On My Head."

Action: Arrow moves to the four numbers.

Props: Numbers 28, 29, 30, and 31.

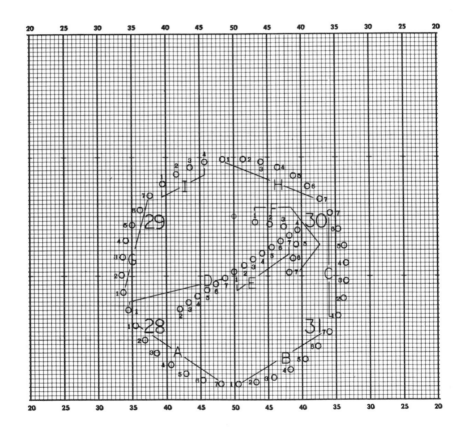

(See page xxvi for Block Band Key to Diagrams.)

12

Basketball and Hoop

Music: "Sweet Georgia Brown," "Jersey Bounce," "A Tisket, A Tasket," "Up, Up and Away."

Action: Basketball moves up and into hoop, optional.

Props: None.

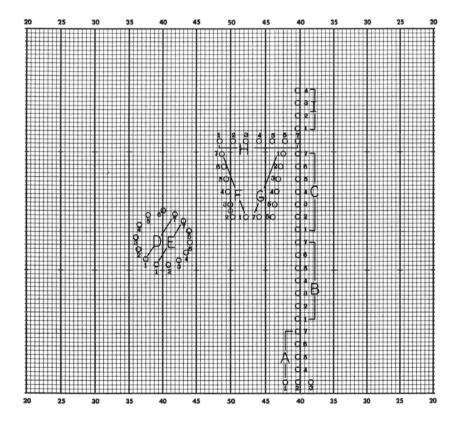

(See page xxvi for Block Band Key to Diagrams.)

13

Bell

Music: "Wake the Town and Tell the People," "The Three Bells," "Winchester Cathedral," "Bells of St. Mary's," "Bells Are Ringing."

Action: Clapper moves right and left, optional.

Props: None.

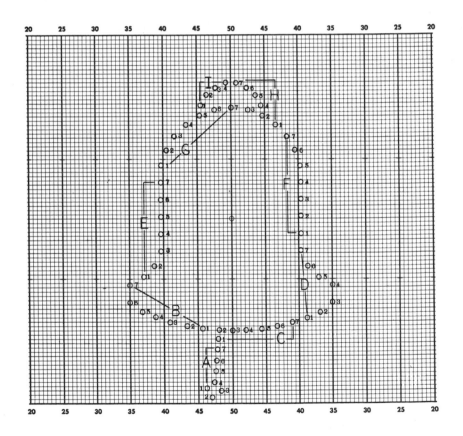

(See page xxvi for Block Band Key to Diagrams.)

Bicycle

Music: "Sidewalks of New York," "Spinning Wheel," "Round and Round," "On a Bicycle Built for Two."

Action: Wheels rotate, optional.

Props: Wheel spokes, optional.

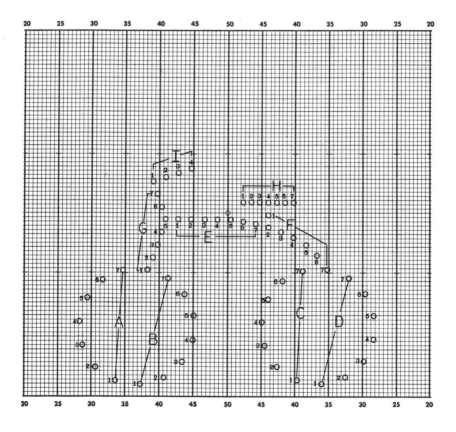

(See page xxvi for Block Band Key to Diagrams.)

15

Bicycle, 1890's

Music: "High Hopes," "The High and the Mighty," "Climb Every Mountain," "Wheel of Fortune," "The Band Played On."

Action: Wheels rotate, optional.

Props: Wheel spokes, optional.

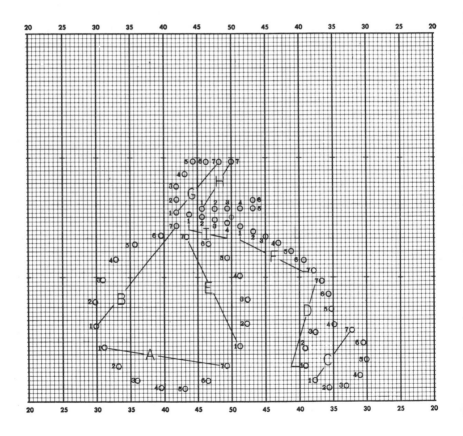

(See page xxvi for Block Band Key to Diagrams.)

16

Birdbath

Music: "Bluebird of Happiness," "Drinking Song," "April Showers," "Sparrow in the Treetop," "Listen to the Mockingbird."

Action: None.

Props: None.

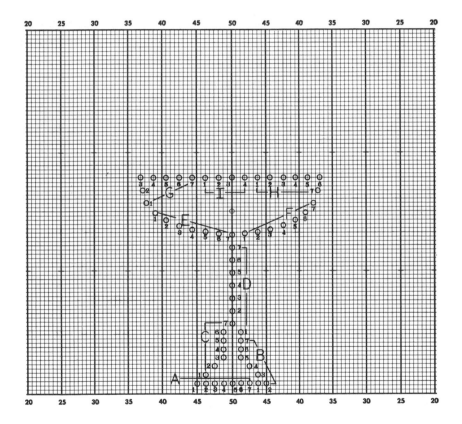

(See page xxvi for Block Band Key to Diagrams.)

17

Birdhouse

Music: "Flamingo," "Hot Canary," "Listen to the Mocking-bird," "Yellow Bird," "Red Wing."

Action: None.

Props: Circular doorway.

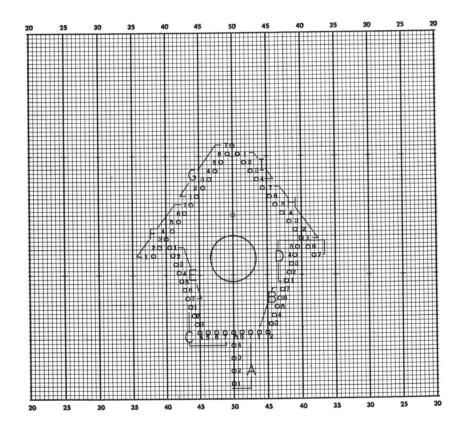

(See page xxvi for Block Band Key to Diagrams.)

Birds, gulls

Music: "Ebb Tide," "On a Clear Day You Can See Forever,"
        "A Sleepy Lagoon," "By the Beautiful Sea."

Action: None.

Props: None.

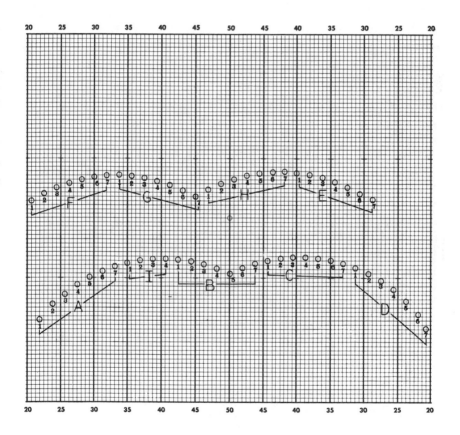

(See page xxvi for Block Band Key to Diagrams.)

19

Blimp

Music: "Around the World in 80 Days," "High Hopes, "Blue Skies," "Up, Up and Away," "It Was a Very Good Year."

Action: Entire formation moves to right, optional.

Props: None.

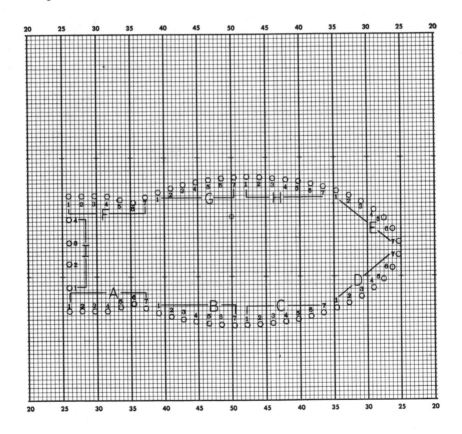

(See page xxvi for Block Band Key to Diagrams.)

Bomb

Music: "There's No Tomorrow," "There I Go," "It's Later Than You Think," "There'll Be Some Changes Made," "All of Me."

Action: None.

Props: None.

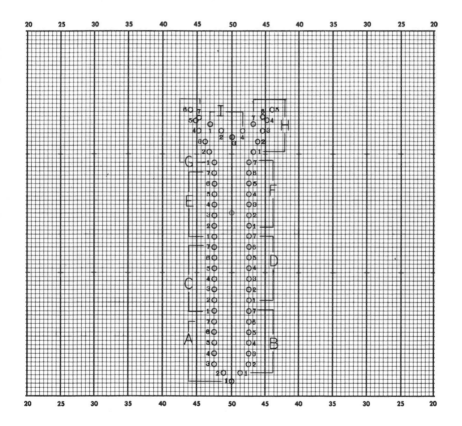

(See page xxvi for Block Band Key to Diagrams.)

Boot

Music: "These Boots Are Made for Walking," "Boots and Saddles," "Shoe Shine Boy," "I'm an Old Cowhand," "Walk on By."

Action: Spur rotates, optional.

Props: Spur.

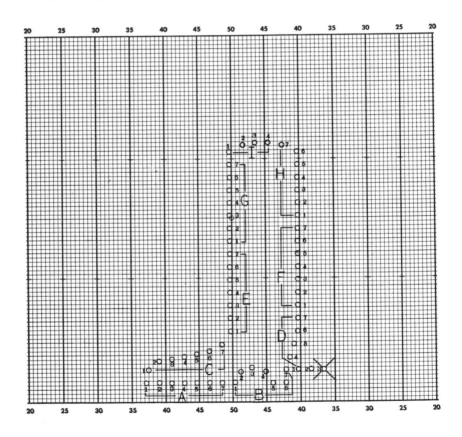

(See page xxvi for Block Band Key to Diagrams.)

Booth, carnival

Music: "Scarborough Fair-Canticle," "Kiss of Fire," "Candy Kisses," "Sugar Lips," "I Kiss Your Hand, Madame."

Action: None.

Props: Two signs.

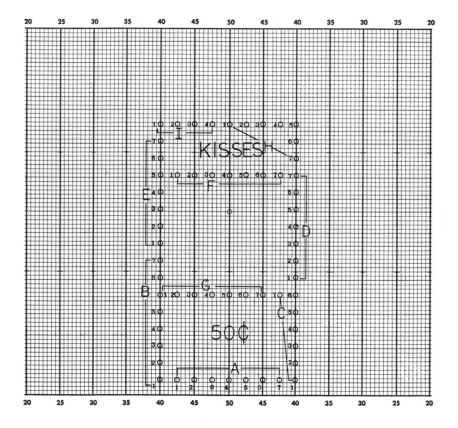

(See page xxvi for Block Band Key to Diagrams.)

Bottle, chemistry

Music: "There'll Be Some Changes Made," "Cocktails for Two," "All Shook Up," "2001 Space Odyssey."

Action: None.

Props: None.

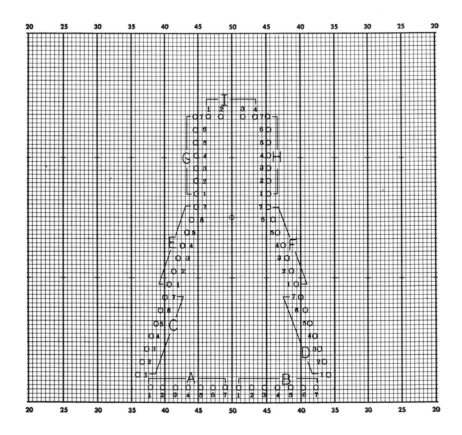

(See page xxvi for Block Band Key to Diagrams.)

Bow and Arrow

Music: "Indian Love Call," "Cherokee," "Ten Little Indians," "Indian Summer," "Zing! Went the Strings of My Heart," "Falling in Love with Love."

Action: String and arrow move to left, optional.

Props: None.

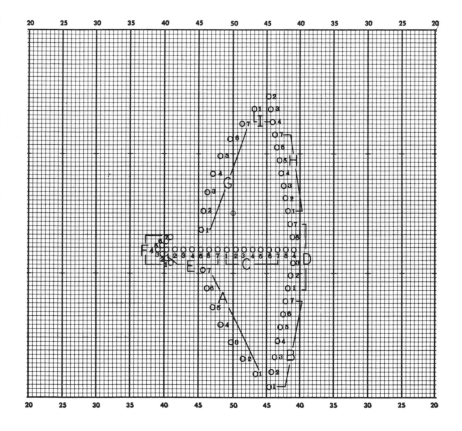

(See page xxvi for Block Band Key to Diagrams.)

Bridge

Music: "Bridge Over the River Kwai," "London Bridge Is Falling Down," "Cross Over the Bridge," "Cry Me a River."

Action: Bridge disintegrates, optional.

Props: None.

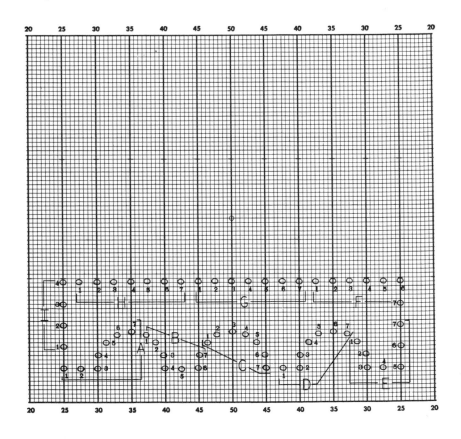

(See page xxvi for Block Band Key to Diagrams.)

Bugler

Music: (any bugle call), "Bugler's Holiday," "Trumpeter's Lullaby," "Man with a Horn," "Strike up the Band," "Sound Off."

Action: None.

Props: None.

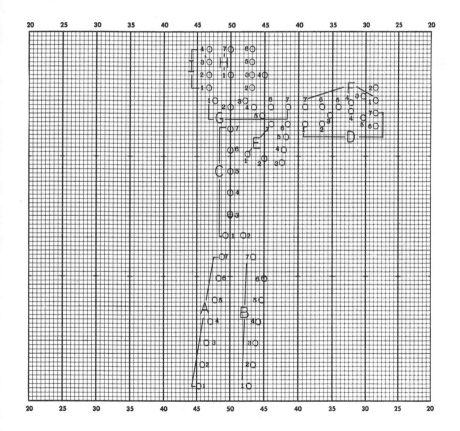

(See page xxvi for Block Band Key to Diagrams.)

Cake

Music: "Anniversary Song," "Anniversary Waltz," "Candy and Cake," "Happy Birthday to You," "If I Knew You Were Comin', I'd 'ave Baked a Cake."

Action: None.

Props: None.

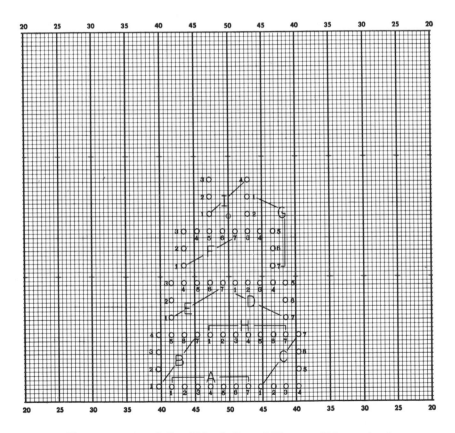

(See page xxvi for Block Band Key to Diagrams.)

Calendar

Music: "It's a Good Day," "Those Were the Days," "It Was a Very Good Year," "Days of Wine and Roses," "Yesterday."

Action: None.

Props: Sign (year, month, or day)

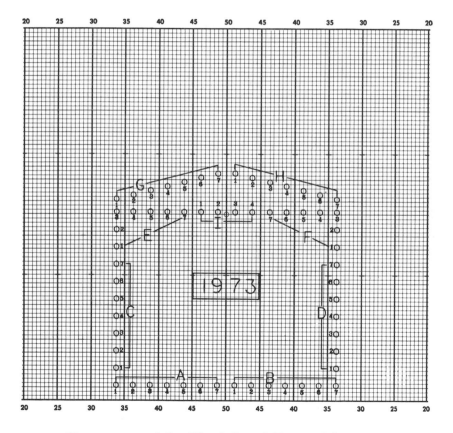

(See page xxvi for Block Band Key to Diagrams.)

Camel

Music: "Desert Song," "Caravan," "How Dry I Am," "Mr. Sandman," "Swingin' Safari," "The Happy Wanderer."

Action: Legs move, optional.

Props: None.

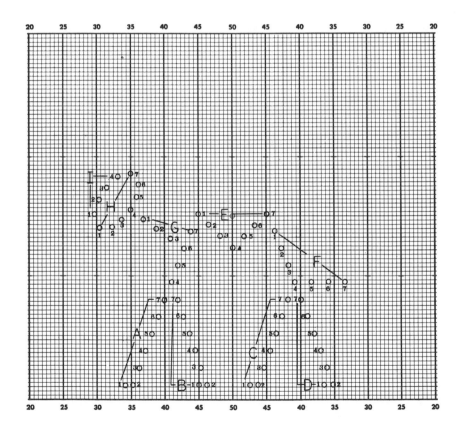

(See page xxvi for Block Band Key to Diagrams.)

30

Camera, T.V.

Music: "Hey, Look Me Over," "Make Believe," "Close to You," "There's No Business Like Show Business," *Pictures from an Exhibition.*

Action: Lens moves to right, optional.

Props: None.

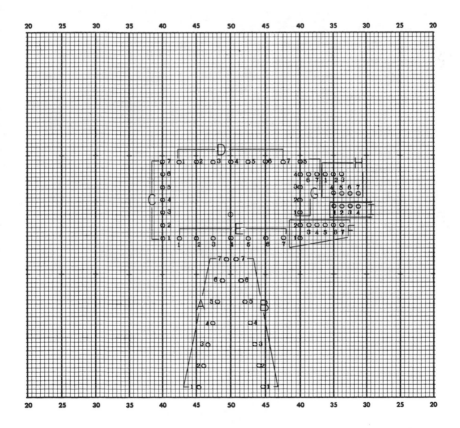

(See page xxvi for Block Band Key to Diagrams.)

Camper

Music: "King of The Road," "North to Alaska," "Route 66," "Home Sweet Home," "California, Here I Come."

Action: Wheels rotate, optional.

Props: Wheel spokes, optional.

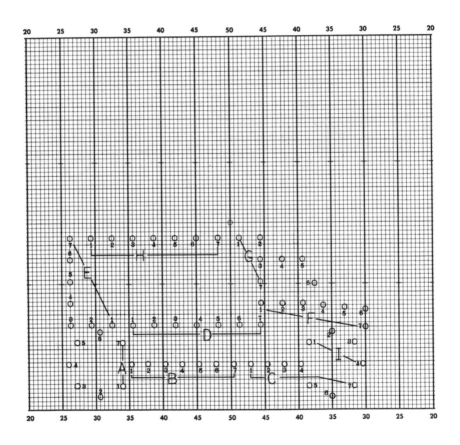

(See page xxvi for Block Band Key to Diagrams.)

Candelabra

Music: "Dinner at Eight," "Strangers in the Night," "Dancing in the Dark," "Smoke Gets in Your Eyes."

Action: None.

Props: None.

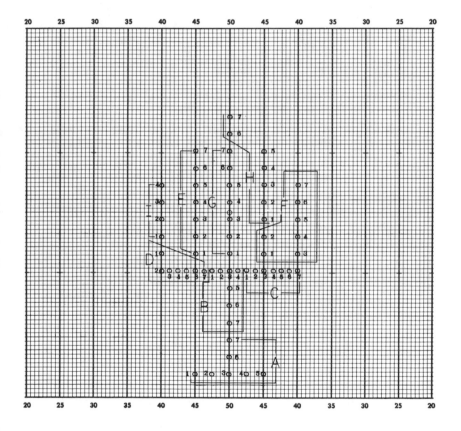

(See page xxvi for Block Band Key to Diagrams.)

Candle

Music: "My Old Flame," "Dinner at Eight," "Dancing in the Dark," "Light My Fire," "The Shadow of Your Smile."

Action: Flame wavers, optional.

Props: None.

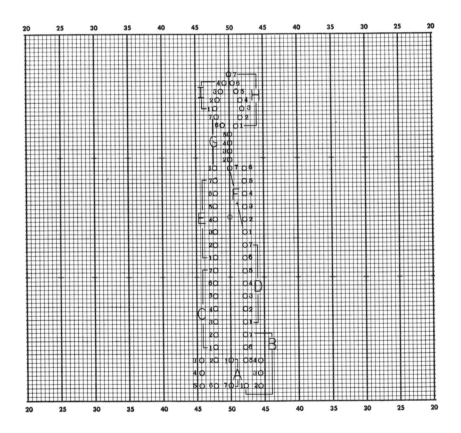

(See page xxvi for Block Band Key to Diagrams.)

Cannon

Music: "Caisson Song," "I Get a Kick Out of You," "Bang Bang," "The British Grenadiers," "Stout Hearted Men."

Action: Wheel rotates, optional.

Props: None.

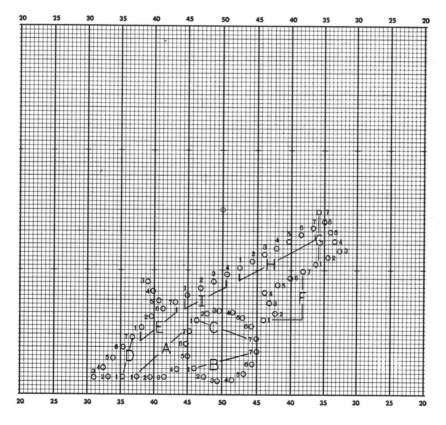

(See page xxvi for Block Band Key to Diagrams.)

Cap, Confederate

Music: "Dixie," "South," "Georgia," "Sweet Georgia Brown," "Marching Through Georgia," "Alabamy Bound," "Mississippi Mud."

Action: None.

Props: None.

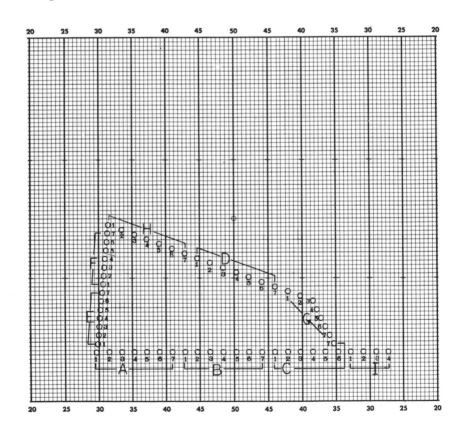

(See page xxvi for Block Band Key to Diagrams.)

Cap, dunce

Music: "What Kind of Fool Am I?" "School Days, School Days," "Fools Rush In," "A Fool Such as I," "Dum Dum," "Slowpoke," "You're Sensational."

Action: None.

Props: None.

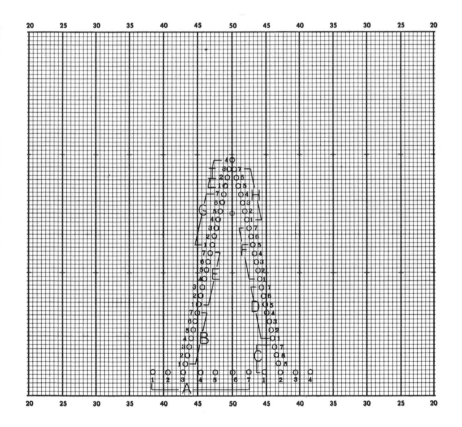

(See page xxvi for Block Band Key to Diagrams.)

Car

Music: "King of the Road," "Chevy Song," "Wipe Out," "Travelin' Man," "In My Merry Oldsmobile."

Action: Wheels rotate, optional.

Props: Wheel spokes, optional.

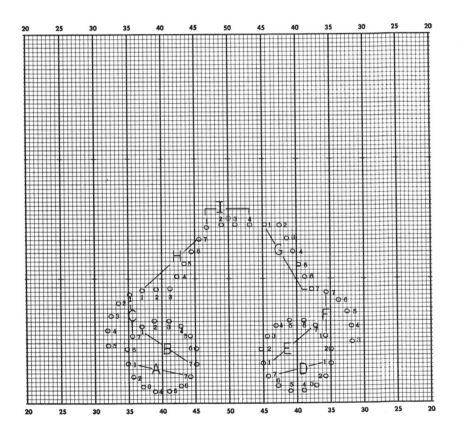

(See page xxvi for Block Band Key to Diagrams.)

Carriage

Music: "Surrey with the Fringe on Top," "Down Yonder," "Memories Are Made of This," "Those Were the Days," "King of the Road," "The Old Grey Mare."

Action: Wheels rotate, carriage moves to right, optional.

Props: Wheel spokes, optional.

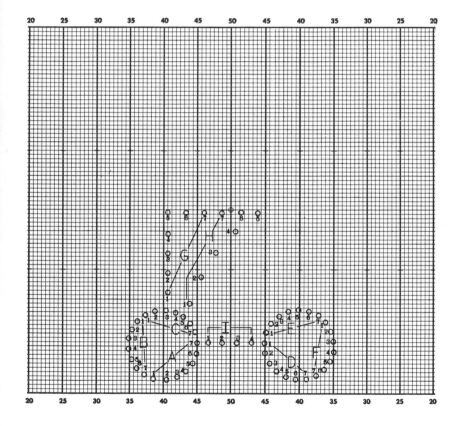

(See page xxvi for Block Band Key to Diagrams.)

39

Carriage, baby

Music: "Baby Face," "Baby Love," "Babes in Toyland," "Walkin' My Baby Back Home," "How Dry I Am."

Action: Wheels rotate, optional.

Props: Wheel spokes, optional.

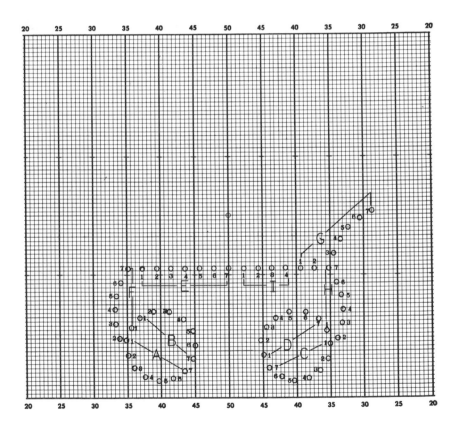

(See page xxvi to Block Band Key to Diagrams.)

Cash Register

Music: "Love For Sale," "Pennies from Heaven," "Penny Lane," "We're in the Money," "Goldfinger," "Green, Green."

Action: Key depresses, optional.

Props: None.

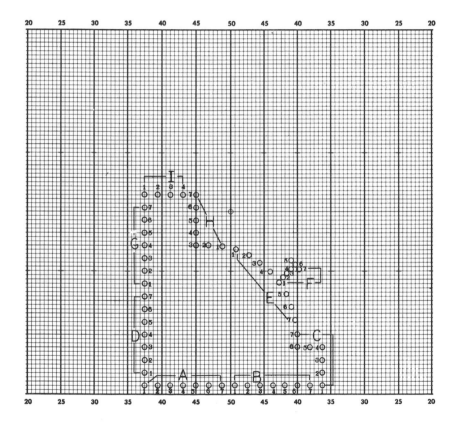

(See page xxvi for Block Band Key to Diagrams.)

41

Castle

Music: "Prisoner of Love," "Some Day My Prince Will Come," "Home Sweet Home," "The Four Walls," "On the Street Where You Live."

Action: None.

Props: None.

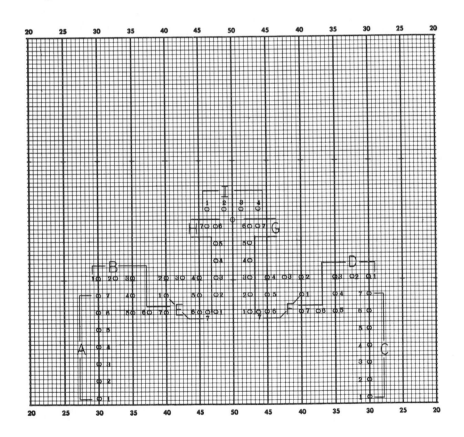

(See page xxvi for Block Band Key to Diagrams.)

Cat

Music: "Pink Panther," "Alley Cat," "Tiger Rag," "The Lion Sleeps Tonight," "Cuddle Up a Little Closer."

Action: Legs and tail move, optional.

Props: Two eyes.

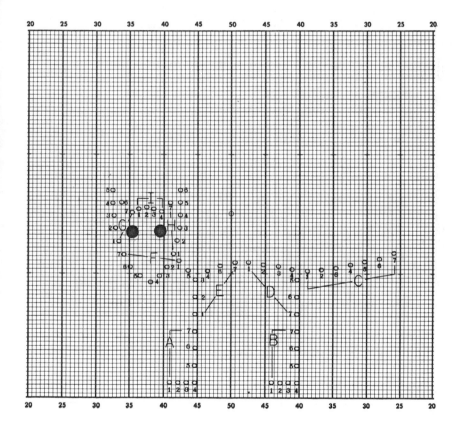

(See page xxvi for Block Band Key to Diagrams.)

Chicken or Turkey

Music: "The Farmer in the Dell," "Turkey in the Straw," "Chicken Reel," "Don't Fence Me In," "A Bushel and a Peck."

Action: Legs move, optional

Props: None.

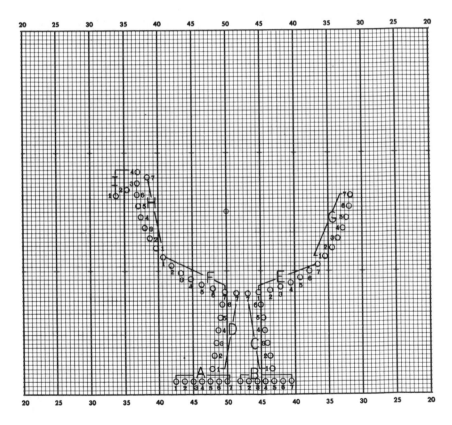

(See page xxvi for Block Band Key to Diagrams.)

Church

Music: "Crusader's Hymn," "The Little Brown Church," "Wedding March," "God Bless America," "Winchester Cathedral," "Wake the Town and Tell the People."

Action: None.

Props: None.

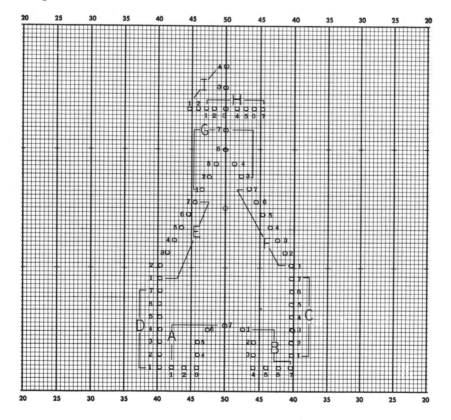

(See page xxvi for Block Band Key to Diagrams.)

45

Cigarette Lighter

Music: "Ritual Fire Dance," "Smoke Gets in Your Eyes," "Puff," "Light My Fire," "Two Cigarettes in the Dark."

Action: Thumb wheel turns, optional.

Props: None.

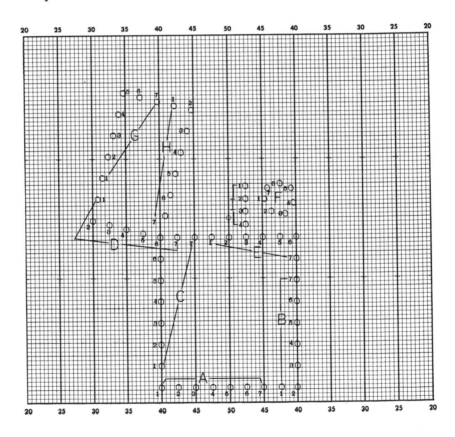

(See page xxvi for Block Band Key to Diagrams.)

46

Cigarette Pack

Music: "Two Cigarettes in the Dark," "Light My Fire," "My Heart Tells Me," "Hot Lips," "Smoke Gets in Your Eyes," "King of the Road."

Action: Cigarettes go into pack, optional.

Props: None.

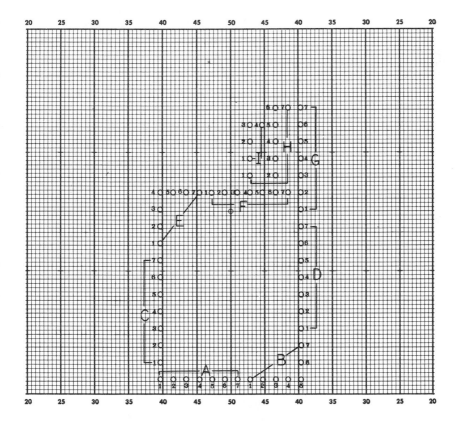

(See page xxvi for Block Band Key to Diagrams.)

47

Clef, bass

Music: "Play a Simple Melody," "But the Melody Lingers On," "Singin' in the Rain," "I Whistle a Happy Tune," "There's Music in the Air," "I Hear a Rhapsody."

Action: None.

Props: None.

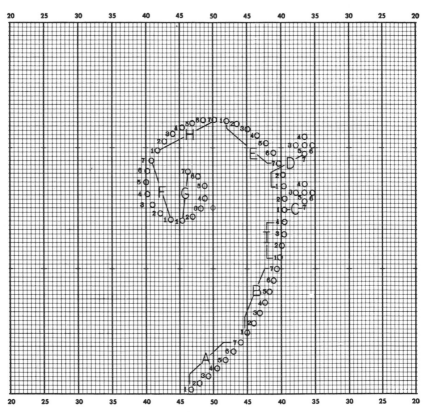

(See page xxvi for Block Band Key to Diagrams.)

Clef, treble

Music: "The Sound of Music," "Strike Up the Band," "Sounds of Silence," "I Hear a Rhapsody," "Music! Music! Music!," "Music to Watch Girls By."

Action: None.

Props: None.

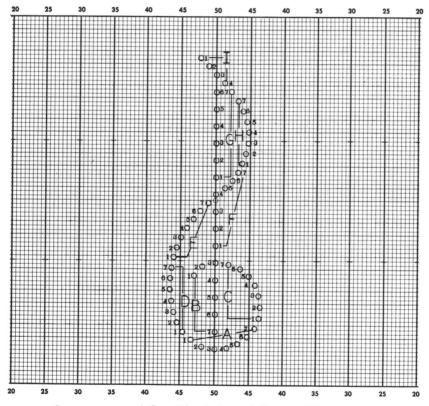

(See page xxvi for Block Band Key to Diagrams.)

Clock

Music: "Syncopated Clock," "Till the End of Time," "As Time Goes By," "Grandfather's Clock," "Now Is the Hour," "Hickory, Dickory Dock."

Action: Hands and pendulum move, optional.

Props: None.

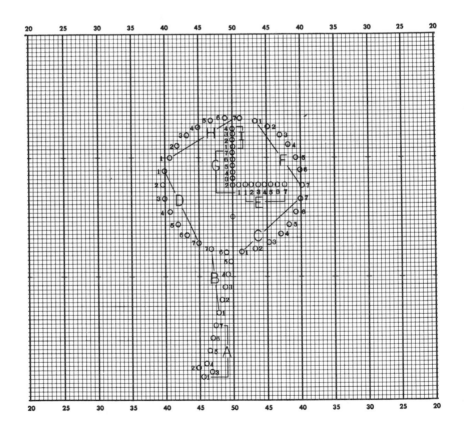

(See page xxvi for Block Band Key to Diagrams.)

Cloud, rain

Music: "Singing in the Rain," "Stormy Weather," "Right as the Rain," "Raindrops Keep Falling on My Head," "Rain."

Action: Drops move to near sideline, optional.

Props: None.

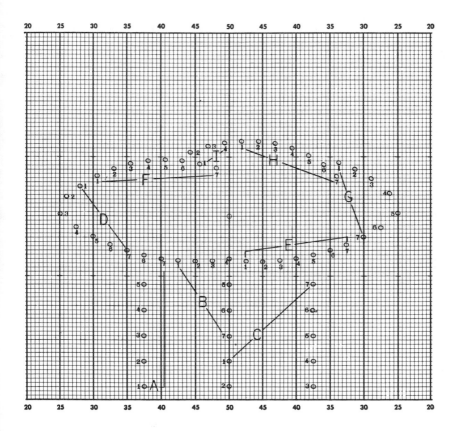

(See page xxvi for Block Band Key to Diagrams.)

Coffeepot

Music: "Java," "Sitting by the Window," "Dinner at Eight,"
         "Drinking Song," "Brazil."

Action: None.

Props: None.

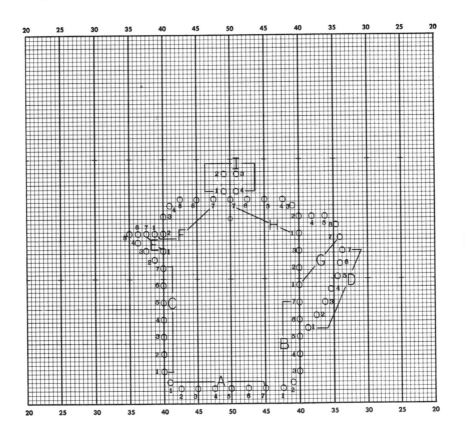

(See page xxvi for Block Band Key to Diagrams.)

Comet

Music: "Catch a Falling Star," "Star Dust," "Swingin' on a Star," "When You Wish Upon a Star," "Starbright."

Action: None.

Props: None.

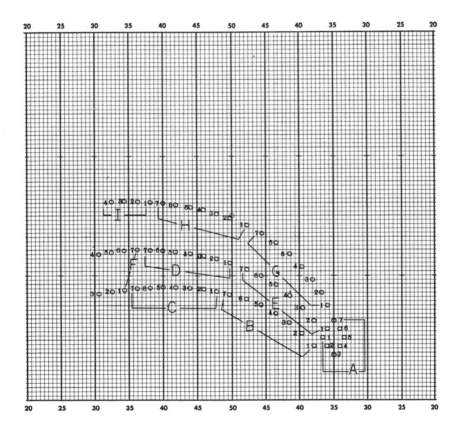

(See page xxvi for Block Band Key to Diagrams.)

Compass

Music: "East of the Sun," "South," "North to Alaska," "How the West Was Won."

Action: Needle moves to the four directions, optional.

Props: Four direction signs.

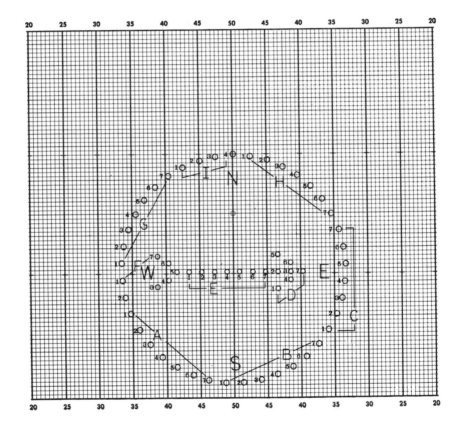

(See page xxvi for Block Band Key to Diagrams.)

Cornet-Trumpet

Music: "Bugler's Holiday," "Trumpeter's Lullaby," "Man with a Horn," "Bugle Call Rag."

Action: Valves go up and down, optional.

Props: None.

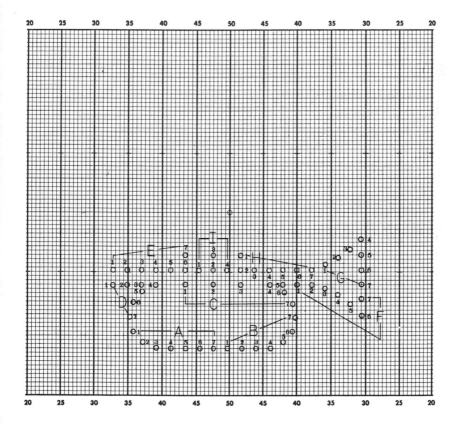

(See page xxvi for Block Band Key to Diagrams.)

Cradle

Music: "Rock-A-Bye Baby," "When My Baby Smiles at Me,"
"Baby Face," "Yes Sir, That's My Baby."

Action: None.

Props: None.

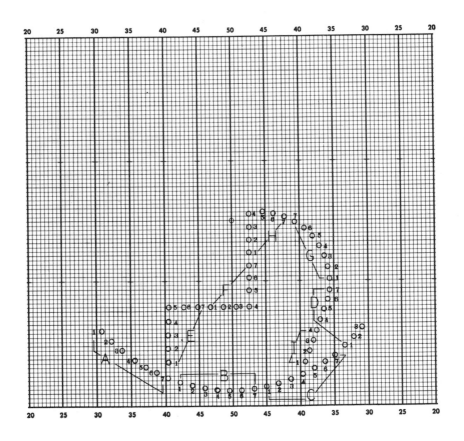

(See page xxvi for Block Band Key to Diagrams.)

56

Croquet Set

Music: "It's All in the Game," "Games People Play," "Hoop-dee-doo," "Green Green Grass of Home." "Back in Your Own Back Yard."

Action: Mallet strikes ball, ball moves through hoop, optional.

Props: None.

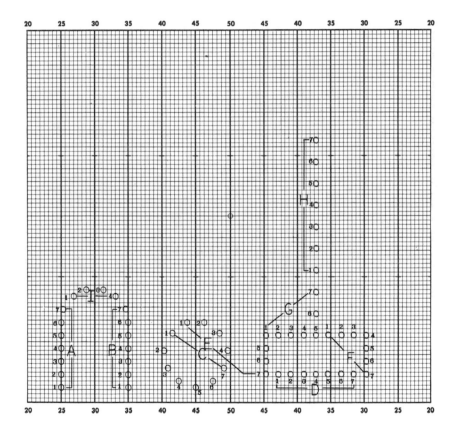

(See page xxvi for Block Band Key to Diagrams.)

57

Cross

Music: "The Old Rugged Cross," "Amen," "Onward Christ-
ian Soldiers," "Holy, Holy, Holy," "He's Got the
Whole World in His Hands."

Action: None.

Props: None.

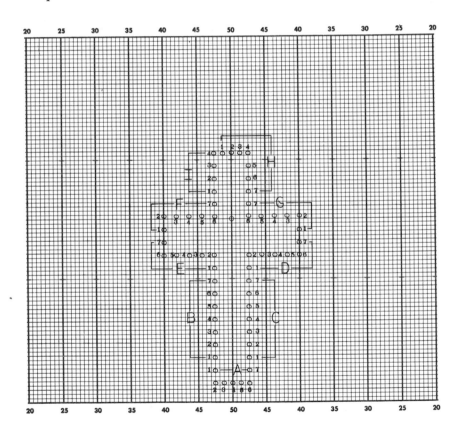

(See page xxvi for Block Band Key to Diagrams.)

Crown

Music: "God Save the Queen," "Coronation March," "Some-day My Prince Will Come," "King of the Road."

Action: None.

Props: None.

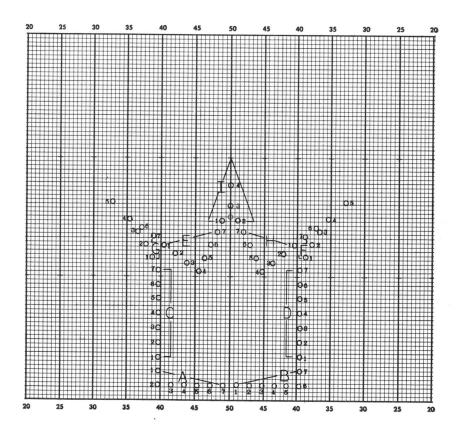

(See page xxvi for Block Band Key to Diagrams.)

Crystal Ball

Music: "Cast Your Fate to the Wind," "Look for the Silver Lining," "Whatever Will Be, Will Be," "I See Your Face Before Me."

Action: None.

Props: None.

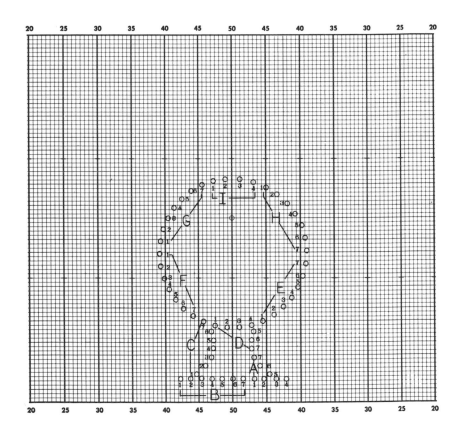

(See page xxvi for Block Band Key to Diagrams.)

Diaper

Music: "There'll Be Some Changes Made," "Rock-A-Bye Baby," "Baby Face," "Babes in Toyland," "When My Baby Smiles at Me."

Action: None.

Props: None.

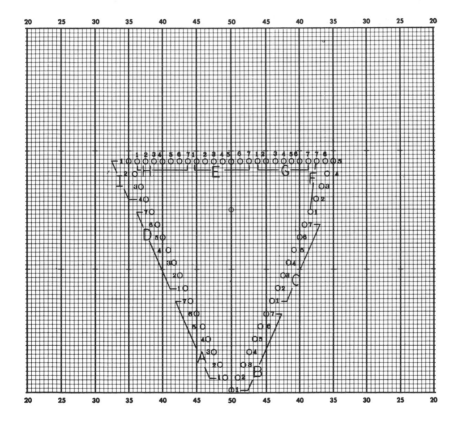

(See page xxvi for Block Band Key to Diagrams.)

Dice

Music: "One O'Clock Jump," "Takes Two to Tango," "Three Coins in the Fountain," "Four Walls," "Five Minutes More."

Action: Add pips one by one, until five are in formation.

Props: Five pips (black circles).

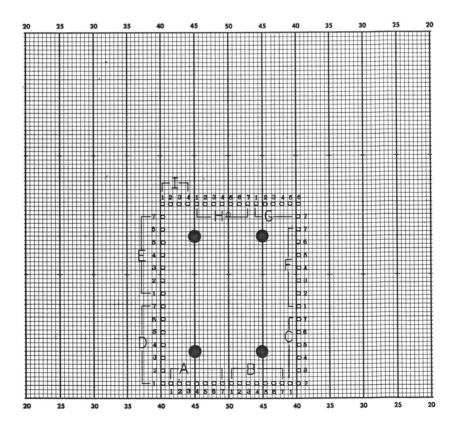

(See page xxvi for Block Band Key to Diagrams.)

Dinosaur

Music: "Talk to the Animals," "Nature Boy," "Walk on By,"
        "Alley Oop," "How Great Thou Art."

Action: Legs, head and tail move, optional.

Props: None.

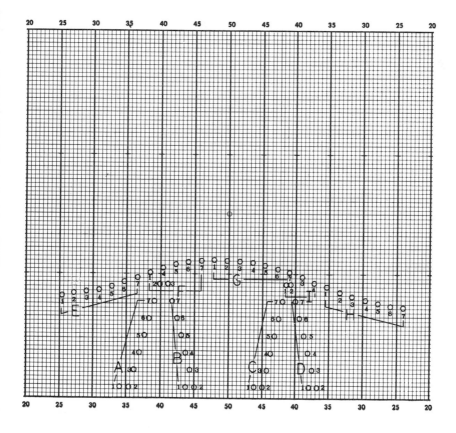

(See page xxvi for Block Band Key to Diagrams.)

Diving Board

Music: "I Cover the Waterfront," "The Swan," "Surfin' Safari," "High Hopes," "Back in Your Own Back Yard," "One O'Clock Jump," "In the Good Old Summer Time."

Action: Board springs, optional.

Props: None.

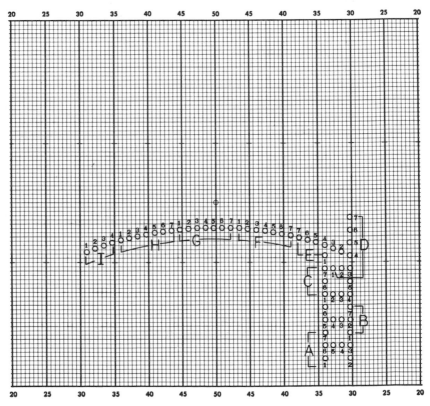

(See page xxvi for Block Band Key to Diagrams.)

Dog

Music: "That Doggie in the Window," "You Ain't Nothin'
but a Hound Dog," "Where, O Where Has My Little
Dog Gone?" "Walkin' My Baby Back Home," "Standing on the Corner."

Action: Legs and tail move, optional.

Props: None.

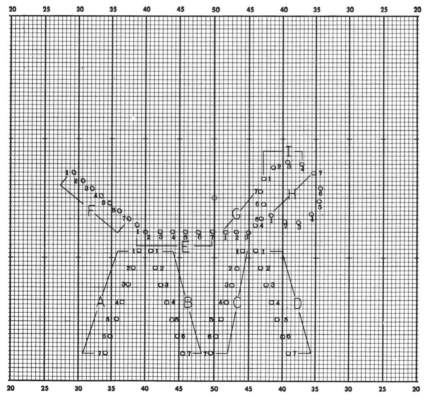

(See page xxvi for Block Band Key to Diagram.)

Dollar Sign

Music: "We're in the Money," "From Rags to Riches," "Poor People of Paris," "Pennies from Heaven."

Action: None.

Props: None.

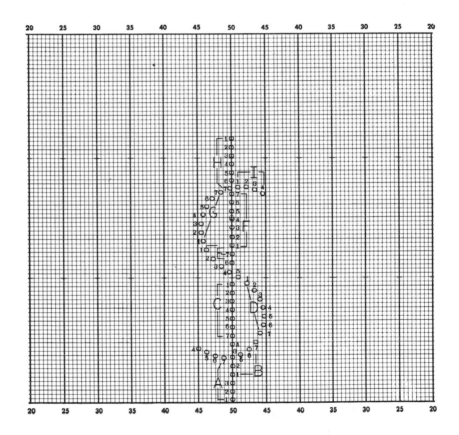

(See page xxvi for Block Band Key to Diagrams.)

Doll House

Music: "Make Believe," "The Doll Dance," "Kewpie Doll," "Yes Sir, That's My Baby," "Dance of the Paper Dolls."

Action: None.

Props: None.

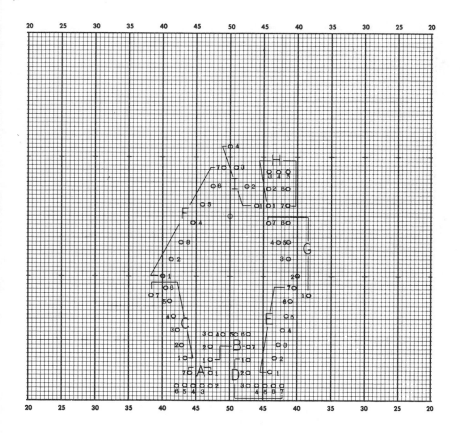

(See page xxvi for Block Band Key to Diagrams.)

Drawing Board

Music: "In an Eighteenth Century Drawing Room," "Teach Me Tonight," "Ramblin' Wreck from Georgia Tech," "Wichita Lineman."

Action: T-square moves up and down, optional.

Props: None.

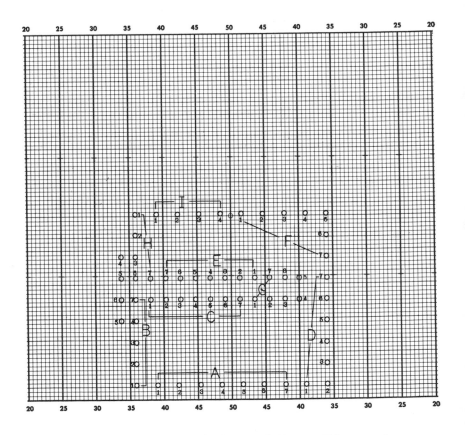

(See page xxvi for Block Band Key to Diagram.)

Drum

Music: "Little Drummer Boy," "The Beat Goes On," "I Got Rhythm," "Hawaiian War Chant," "Drums in My Heart."

Action: None.

Props: None.

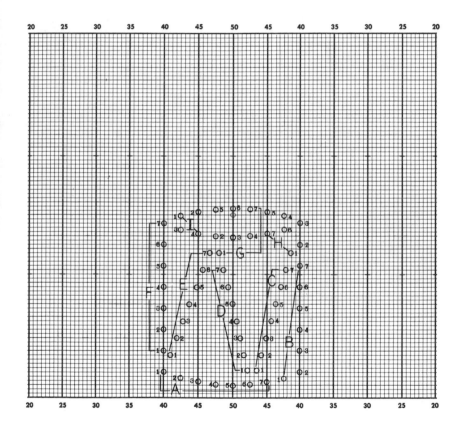

(See page xxvi for Block Band Key to Diagram.)

Easel, canvas

Music: "Love Is Blue," "Mona Lisa," "Paint Your Wagon," "Paint It Black," "My Coloring Book," *Pictures from an Exhibition.*

Action: None.

Props: None.

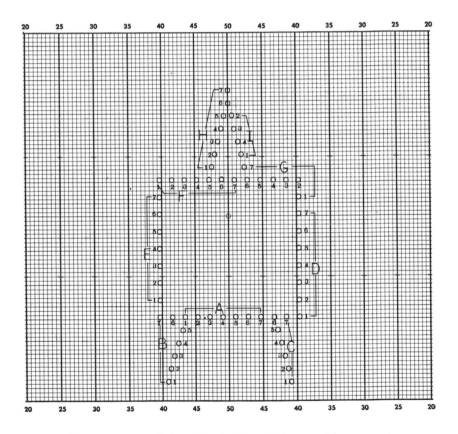

(See page xxvi for Block Band Key to Diagrams.)

Eiffel Tower

Music: "April in Paris," "I Love Paris," "The Poor People of Paris," "Mam'selle," "Ballet Parisien."

Action: None.

Props: None.

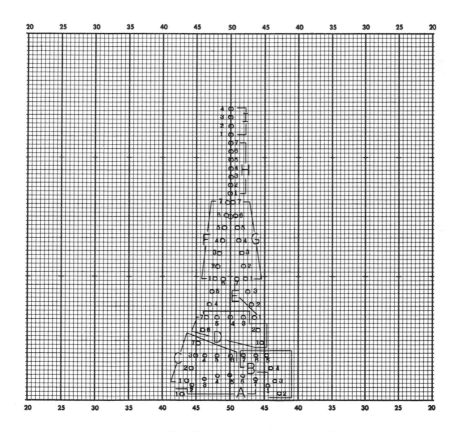

(see page xxvi for Block Band Key to Diagrams.)

Envelope

Music: "Tammy," "Please Mr. Postman," "Send for Me,"
"Love Letters in the Sand," "To Sir with Love," "Sincerely," "A Dear John Letter."

Action: None.

Props: A sign with a name on it.

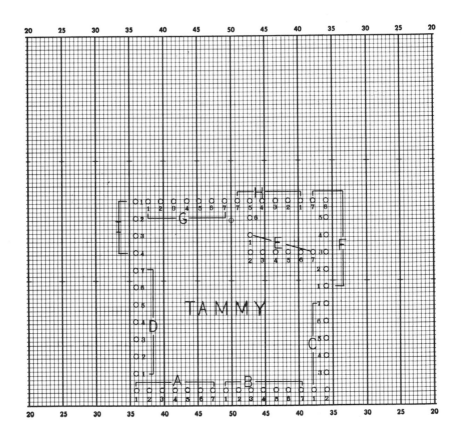

(See page xxvi for Block Band Key to Diagrams.)

Eyes

Music: "Spanish Eyes," "Hey, Look Me Over," "On a Clear Day You Can See Forever," "I'll Be Seeing You."

Action: Eyeballs move right and left, optional.

Props: Two circles for eyeballs.

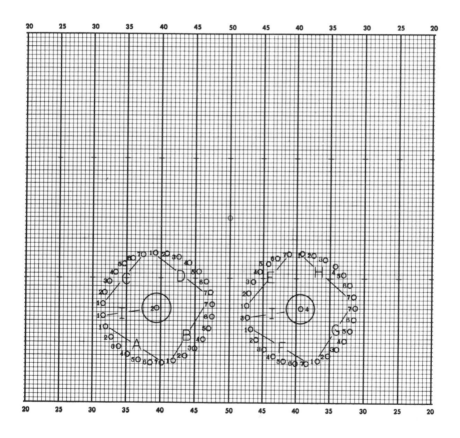

(See page xxvi for Block Band Key to Diagrams.)

73

Face, happy

Music: "The Shadow of Your Smile," "Put On a Happy Face," "Smilin' Through," "The Happy Wanderer," "Oh, Happy Day."

Action: Eyes move, optional.

Props: Two circles for eyes.

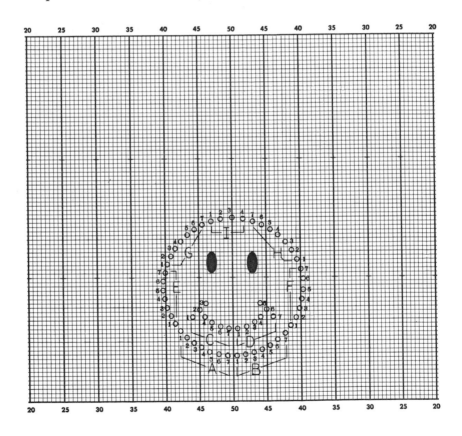

(See page xxvi for Block Band Key to Diagrams.)

Face, sad

Music: "Cry Me a River," "Nobody Knows de Trouble I've Seen," "Blue Monday," "I Ain't Got Nobody."

Action: Eyes move, optional.

Props: Two circles for eyes.

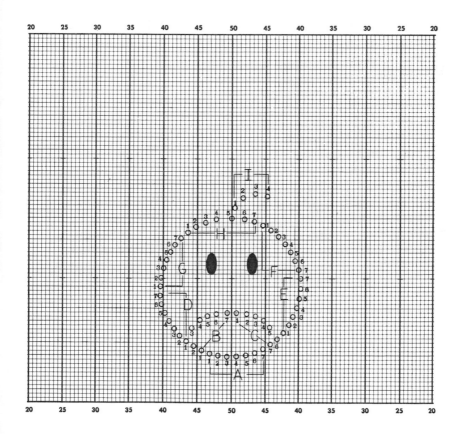

(See page xxvi for Block Band Key to Diagrams.)

75

Fan, Spanish

Music: "Spanish Eyes," "The Lonely Bull," "In a Little Spanish Town," "Lady of Spain," "April in Portugal."

Action: None.

Props: None.

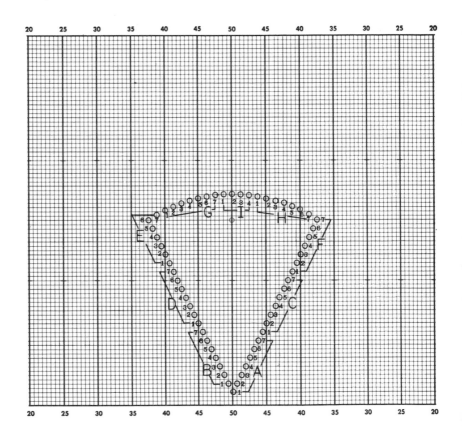

(See page xxvi for Block Band Key to Diagrams.)

Ferris Wheel

Music: "Round and Round," "You Go to My Head," "Carousel," "Meet Me in St. Louis, Louis."

Action: Wheel rotates, optional.

Props: None.

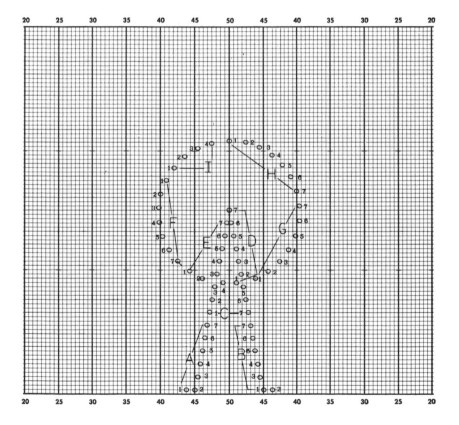

(See page xxvi for Block Band Key to Diagrams.)

Fishing Pole

Music: "Gone Fishin'," "In The Good Old Summer Time," "Lazy Bones," "Summertime," "Cruising Down the River."

Action: Fish goes towards pole tip, optional.

Props: Fishline.

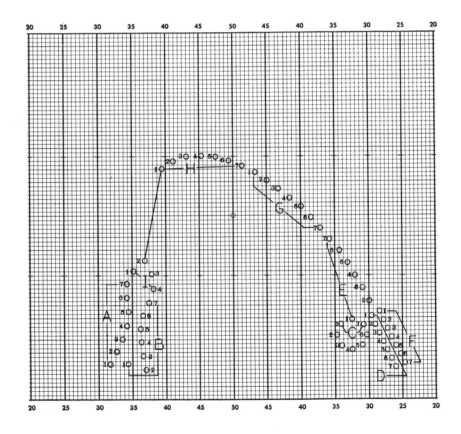

(See page xxvi for Block Band Key to Diagrams.)

Flag

Music: "America," "This Is My Country," "American Patrol," "Battle Hymn of the Republic," "God Bless America."

Action: None.

Props: None.

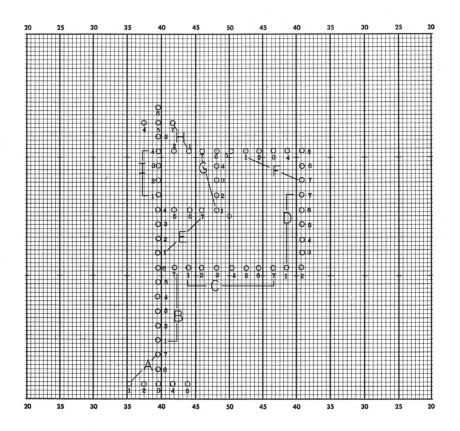

(See page xxvi for Block Band Key to Diagrams.)

Flower

Music: "Sweet Violets," "Red Roses for a Blue Lady," "One Dozen Roses," "Roses Are Red," "Tiptoe, Through the Tulips."

Action: None.

Props: None.

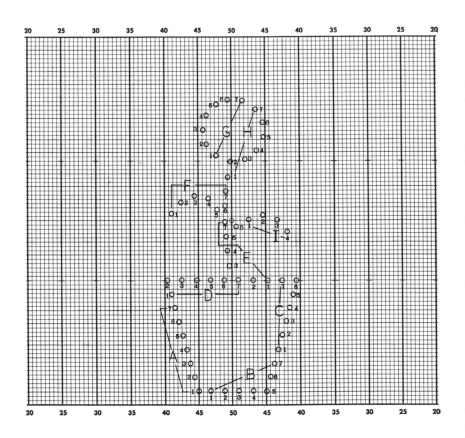

(See page xxvi for Block Band Key to Diagrams.)

Fountain

Music: "Three Coins in the Fountain," "Love Is a Many-Splendored Thing," "Rhythm of the Rain," "I Love Paris."

Action: None.

Props: None.

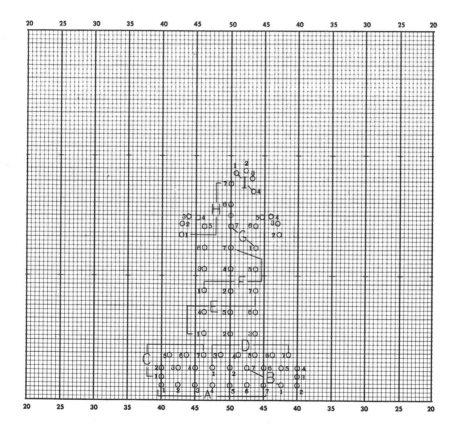

(See page xxvi for Block Band Key to Diagrams.)

Four-H

Music: "He's Got the Whole World in His Hands," "Heart," "Heartaches," "You Go to My Head," "I Feel Good, I Feel Fine."

Action: None.

Props: None.

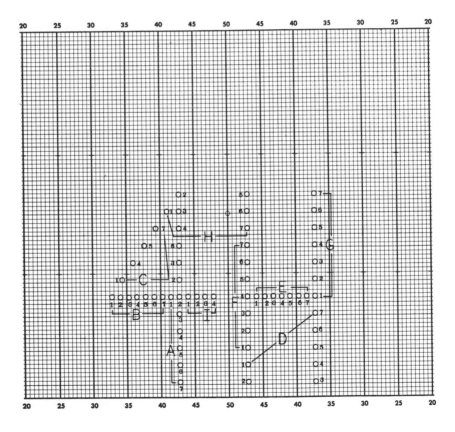

(See page xxvi for Block Band Key to Diagrams.)

Four Leaf Clover

Music: "Mr. Lucky," "Lucky in Love," "I'm Looking Over a Four Leaf Clover," "Too-ra-loo-ra-loo-ral."

Action: None.

Props: None.

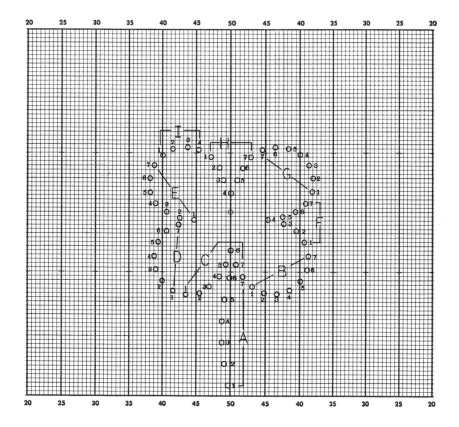

(See page xxvi for Block Band Key to Diagrams.)

Gibraltar

Music: "Rock of Ages," "The British Grenadiers," "Rock Around the Clock," "Rock and Roll Waltz," "Rule, Brittania."

Action: None.

Props: None.

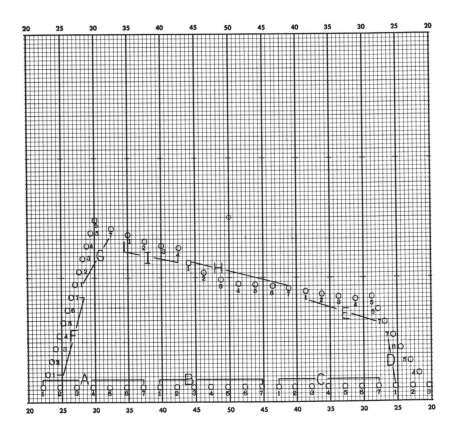

(See page xxvi for Block Band Key to Diagrams.)

84

Girl

Music: "Georgy Girl," "The Girl That I Marry," "Girl of My Dreams," "Music to Watch Girls By," "I Want a Girl," "Laura," "Josephine."

Action: None.

Props: None.

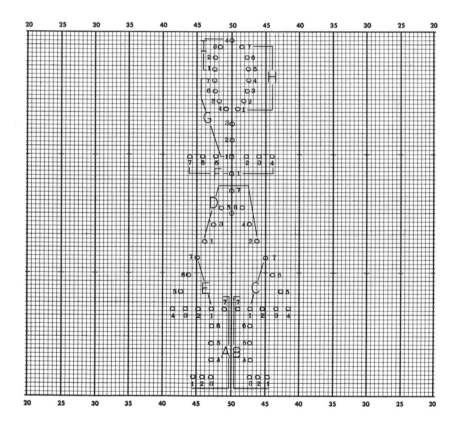

(See page xxvi for Block Band Key to Diagrams.)

Glass

Music: "Cool, Cool Water," "Drinking Song," "Cocktails for Two," "Rum and Coca-Cola."

Action: None.

Props: None.

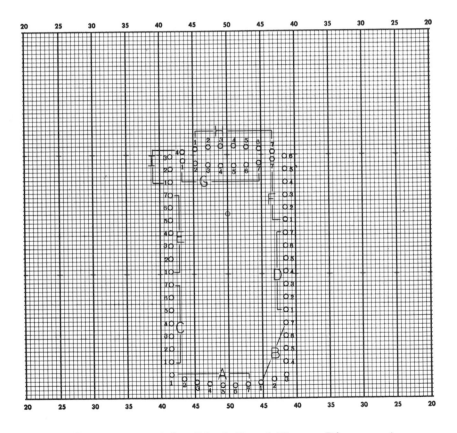

(See page xxvi for Block Band Key to Diagrams.)

Glass, wine

Music: "Days of Wine and Roses," "Blue Champagne," "Here's to Romance," "Wine, Woman and Song," "Drink to Me Only with Thine Eyes."

Action: None.

Props: None.

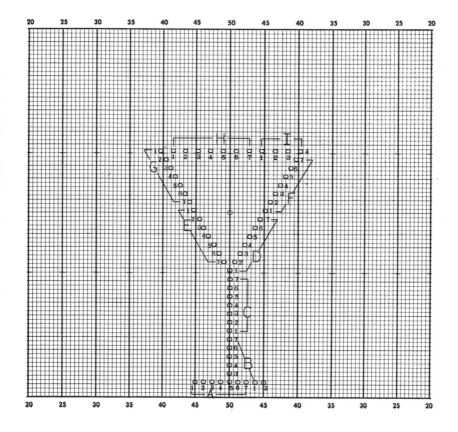

(See page xxvi for Block Band Key to Diagrams.)

Globe

Music: "Around the World in 80 Days," "I'm Sitting on Top of the World," "A World Without Love," "One World," *New World* Symphony themes," "What the World Needs Now Is Love."

Action: None.

Props: Equator line.

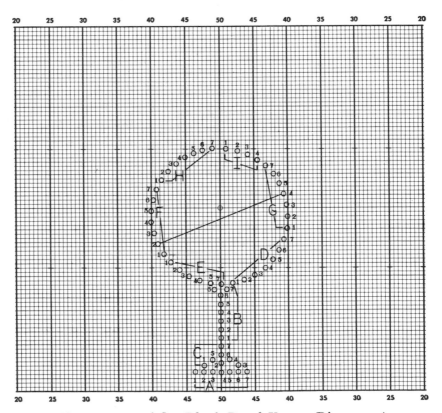

(See page xxvi for Block Band Key to Diagrams.)

Goalpost

Music: "Gillette Look Sharp March," "I Get a Kick Out of You," "Over and Over," "Buckle Down, Winsocki," "Put Your Arms Around Me, Honey."

Action: None.

Props: None.

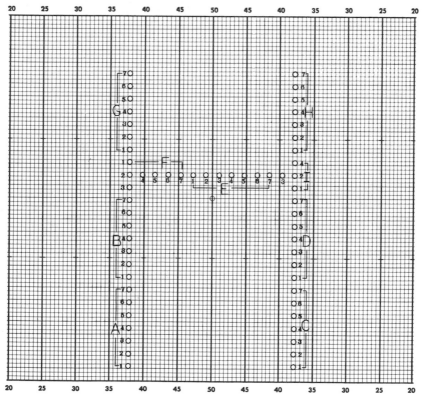

(See page xxvi for Block Band Key to Diagrams.)

Gondola

Music: "Cruising Down the River," "Drifting and Dreaming," "Barcarolle," "Carnival of Venice" (theme).

Action: None.

Props: None.

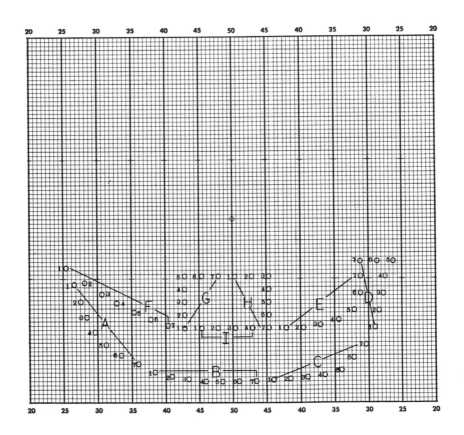

(See page xxvi for Block Band Key to Diagrams.)

90

Guillotine

Music: "You Go to My Head," "Goin' Out of My Head," "Take It Easy," "I Ain't Got Nobody," "I Almost Lost My Mind," "A Tisket, A Tasket."

Action: Blade (G rank) descends, optional.

Props: None.

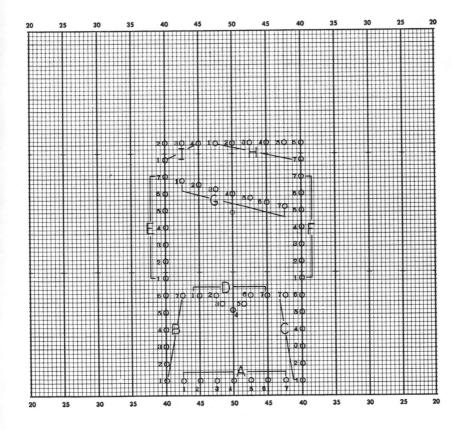

(See page xxvi for Block Band Key to Diagrams.)

Hangman's Noose

Music: "Five Minutes More," "Till the End of Time," "The Hanging Tree," "Walk, Don't Run," "I'll String Along with You."

Action: Noose swings, optional.

Props: None.

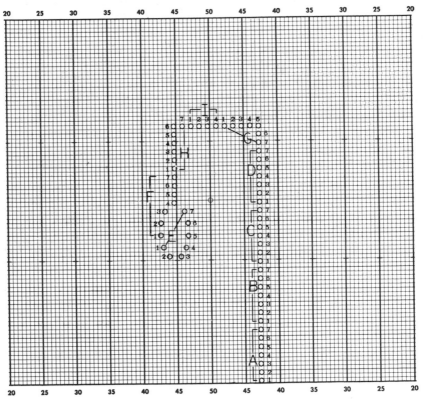

(See page xxvi for Block Band Key to Diagrams.)

Harp

Music: "Holiday for Strings," "Zing! Went the Strings of My Heart," "I'll String Along with You," "The Harp That Once, Thro' Tara's Halls," "Love Is a Many-Splendored Thing."

Action: None.

Props: Several strings, optional.

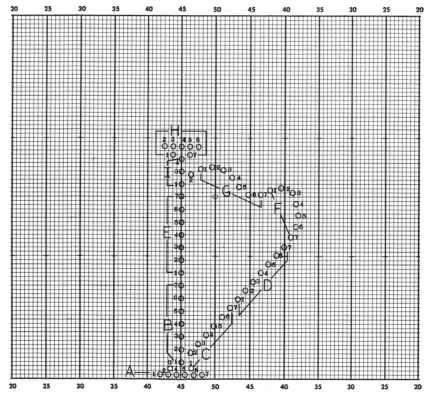

(See page xxvi for Block Band Key to Diagrams.)

Hat, cowboy

Music: "Home on the Range," "Red River Valley," "Tumbling Tumbleweeds," "Down in the Valley," "High Noon," "The Magnificent Seven."

Action: None.

Props: None.

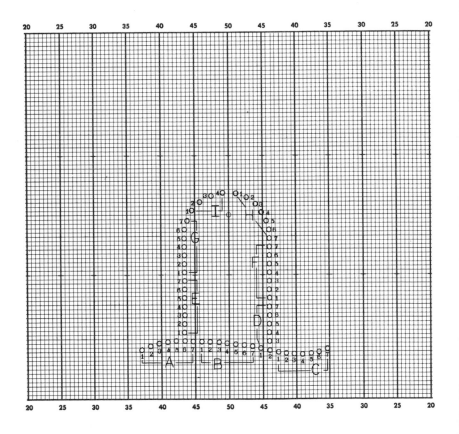

(See page xxvi for Block Band Key to Diagrams.)

Hat, sailor

Music: "Ebb Tide," "Anchors Aweigh," *Victory at Sea* (themes), "Downtown," "Shrimp Boats," "Row, Row, Row Your Boat."

Action: None.

Props: None.

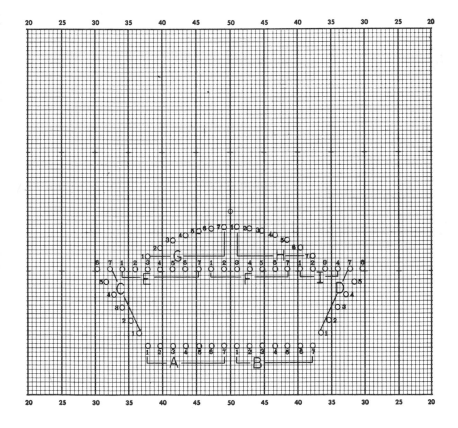

(See page xxvi for Block Band Key to Diagrams.)

Heart

Music: "Heartaches," "Heart of My Heart," "Your Cheatin' Heart," "P.S., I Love You," "My Heart Cries for You."

Action: Arrow moves through heart, optional.

Props: None.

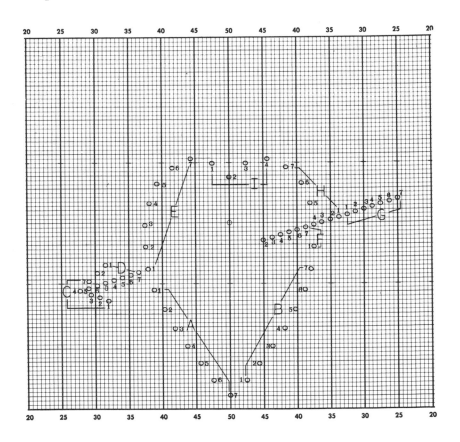

(See page xxvi for Block Band Key to Diagrams.)

Horse

Music: "Ghost Riders in the Sky," "Strawberry Roan," "I'm an Old Cowhand," "I'm Headin' for the Last Round-up."

Action: Legs move, optional.

Props: None.

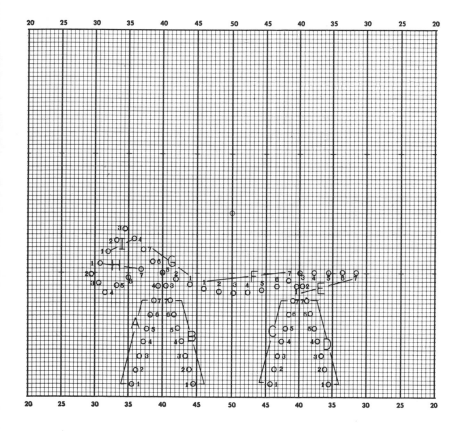

(See page xxvi for Block Band Key to Diagrams.)

Hourglass

Music: "Till the End of Time," "Now Is the Hour," "Time on My Hands," "Wake Up and Live."

Action: Sand level descends.

Props: None.

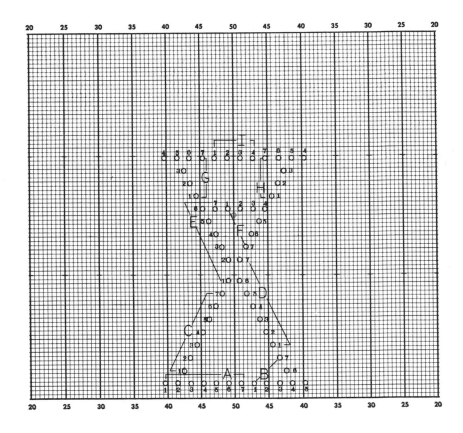

(See page xxvi for Block Band Key to Diagrams.)

House

Music: "This Old House," "Home Sweet Home," "On the Street Where You Live," "House of the Rising Sun."

Action: None.

Props: None.

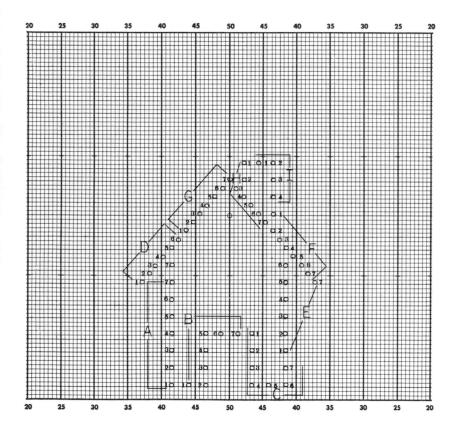

(See page xxvi for Block Band Key to Diagrams.)

Hypodermic Needle

Music: "I've Got You Under My Skin," "You Always Hurt the One You Love," "My Heart Cries for You," "I'll Never Smile Again," "Heartaches."

Action: Plunger and needle move to right, optional.

Props: None.

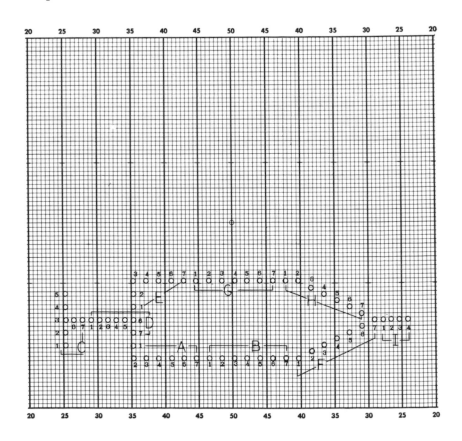

(See page xxvi for Block Band Key to Diagrams.)

Igloo

Music: "Snow Bird," "North to Alaska," "Winter Wonderland," "Cold, Cold Heart."

Action: None.

Props: None.

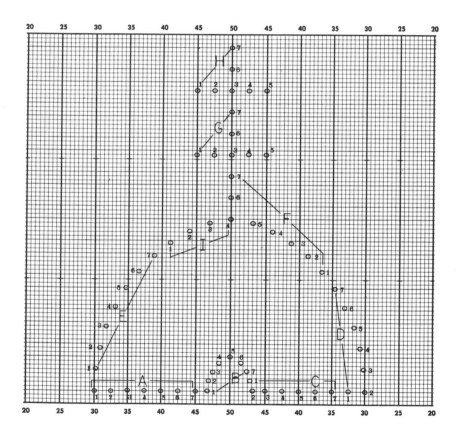

(See page xxvi for Block Band Key to Diagrams.)

Kite

Music: "Windy," "The Breeze and I," "I'm Sitting on Top of the World," "Up, Up and Away," "I'll String Along with You."

Action: Tail flutters, optional.

Props: Kite string.

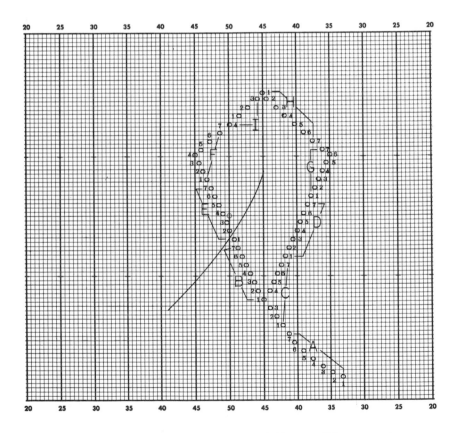

(See page xxvi for Block Band Key to Diagrams.)

Lawn Mower

Music: "Green Grass of Home," "Back in Your Own Back Yard," "Green, Green," "It's So Nice to Have a Man Around the House."

Action: Wheels and/or entire formation moves to right, optional.

Props: None.

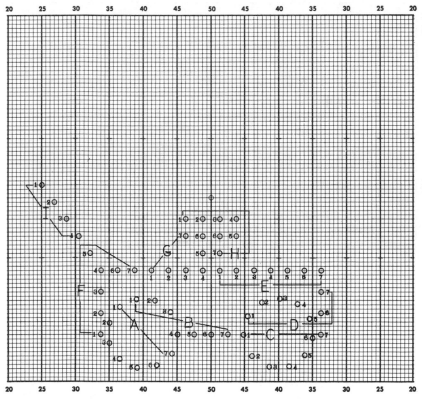

(See page xxvi for Block Band Key to Diagrams.)

103

Leaf

Music: "Autumn Leaves," "Little Green Apples," "Cherry Pink and Apple Blossom White," "The Tree in the Meadow," "Green Green Grass of Home."

Action: None.

Props: None.

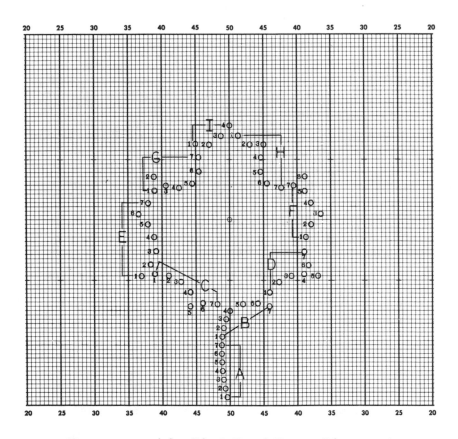

(See page xxvi for Block Band Key to Diagrams.)

Lectern

Music: "Teach Me Tonight," "School Days, School Days," "Harper Valley P.T.A.," "I'd Like to Teach the World to Sing."

Action: None.

Props: None.

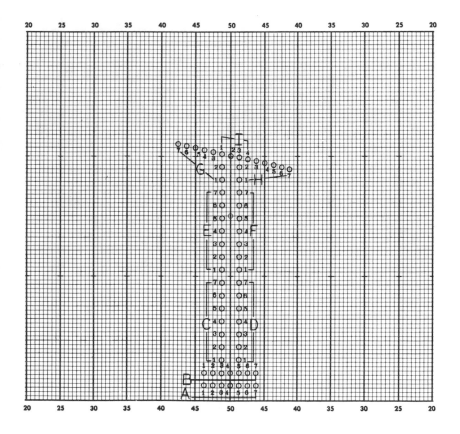

(See page xxvi for Block Band Key to Diagrams.)

Light, traffic

Music: "Walk, Don't Run," "Red Roses for a Blue Lady," "Yellow Bird," "She Wore a Yellow Ribbon," "Green Green Grass of Home."

Action: None.

Props: Three colored circles: red, yellow and green.

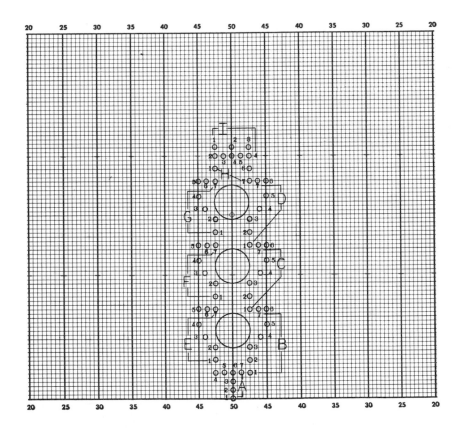

(See page xxvi for Block Band Key to Diagrams.)

Lollipop

Music: "The Candy Man," "Sugarlips," "Candy," "Candy Kisses," "Sweet and Lovely," "On the Good Ship, Lollipop."

Action: None.

Props: None.

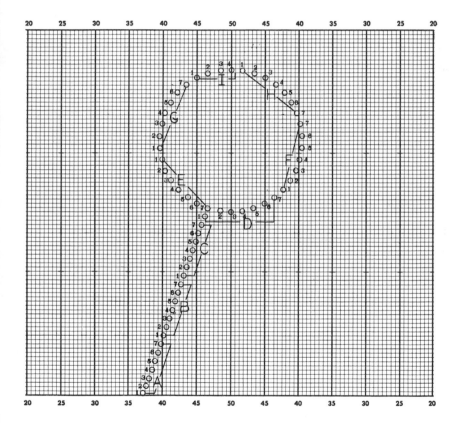

(See page xxvi for Block Band Key to Diagrams.)

107

Machine Gun

Music: "Round and Round," "Peter Gunn," "Marine's Hymn," "I Cover the Waterfront," "Heartaches," "Something's Gotta Give."

Action: Gun part swivels, optional.

Props: None.

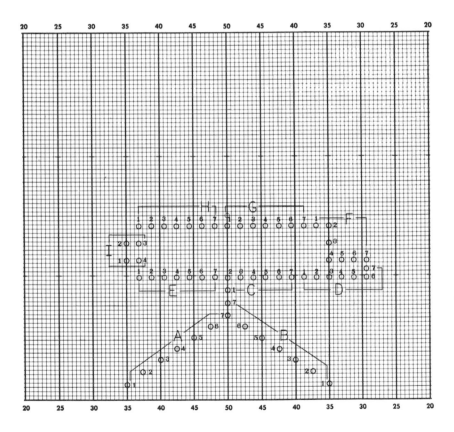

(See page xxvi for Block Band Key to Diagrams.)

Mailbox

Music: "Please Mr. Postman," "Love Letters in the Sand," "Send for Me," "P.S. I Love You," "Sincerely."

Action: None.

Props: None.

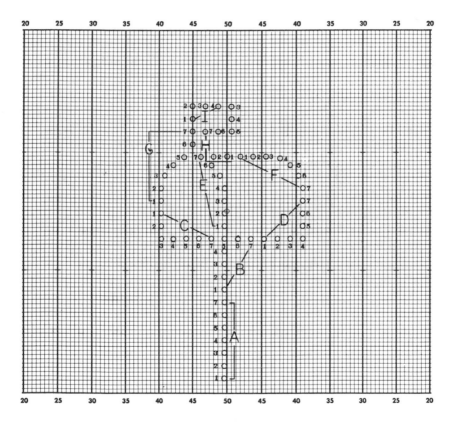

(See page xxvi for Block Band Key to Diagrams.)

Match

Music: "Smoke Gets in Your Eyes," "Two Cigarettes in the Dark," "Light My Fire," "My Old Flame," "I Don't Want to Set the World on Fire."

Action: None.

Props: None.

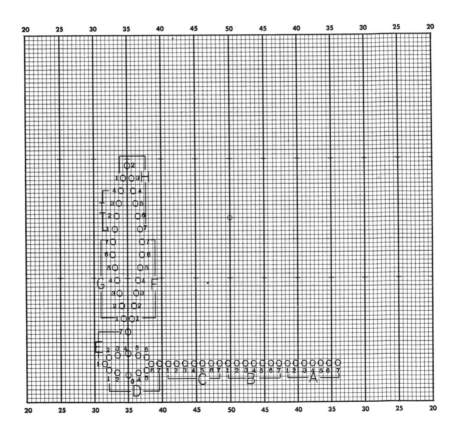

(See page xxvi for Block Band Key to Diagrams.)

Megaphone

Music: "Hey There," "Sound Off," "Together," "Get Together," "On Wisconsin," "Winchester Cathedral."

Action: None.

Props: None.

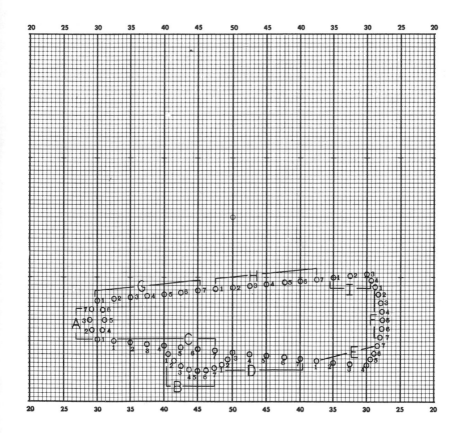

(See page xxvi for Block Band Key to Diagrams.)

Metronome

Music: "I Got Rhythm," "The Beat Goes On," "Syncopated Clock," "Time on My Hands," "Rhythm of the Rain," "Count Every Star."

Action: Pendulum swings back and forth, optional.

Props: None.

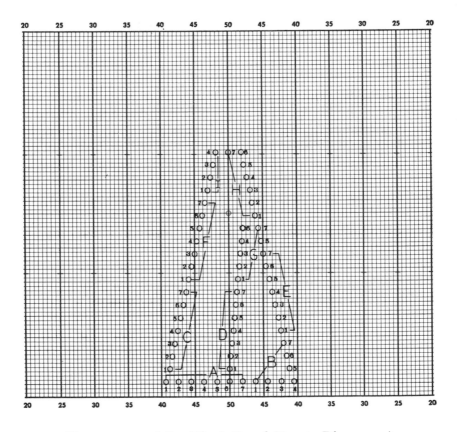

(See page xxvi for Block Band Key to Diagrams.)

Mortarboard

Music: "Teach Me Tonight," "Halls of Ivy," "School Days, School Days," "The Whiffenpoof Song."

Action: Tassle moves from left to right, optional.

Props: None.

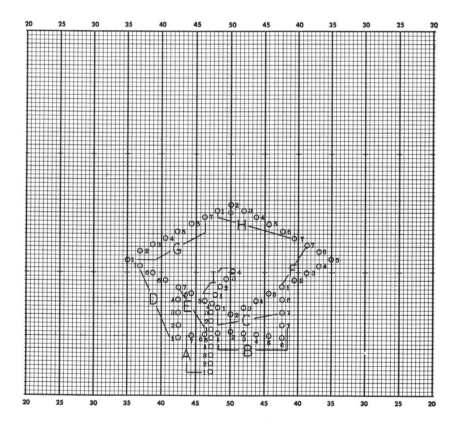

(See page xxvi for Block Band Key to Diagrams.)

Mountains

Music: "Climb Every Mountain," "I'm Sitting on Top of the World," "The High and the Mighty," "High Hopes."

Action: None.

Props: None.

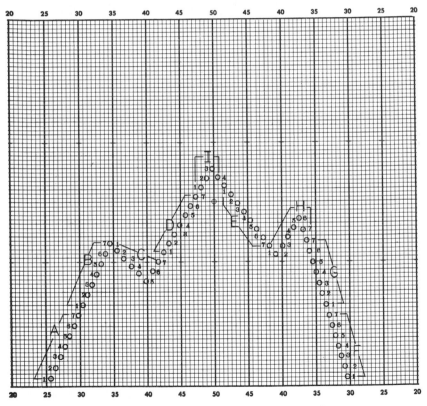

(See page xxvi for Block Band Key to Diagrams.)

Noah's Ark

Music: "Baby Elephant Walk," "Talk to the Animals," "The Day the Rains Came," "Don't Let the Rain Come Down," "Flamingo," "High Hopes," "Takes Two to Tango."

Action: None.

Props: None.

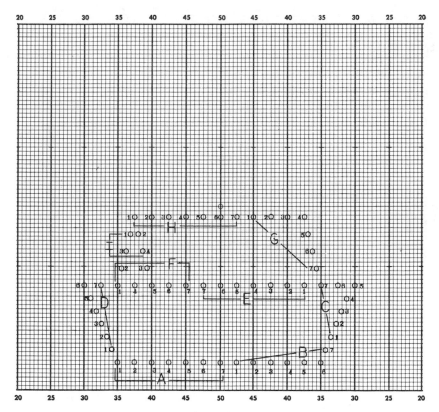

(See page xxvi for Block Band Key to Diagrams.)

115

Notes

Music: "The Sound of Music," "Do-Re-Mi," "Rhapsody in Blue," "Say It with Music," "Music to Watch Girls By," "Music! Music! Music!"

Action: None.

Props: None.

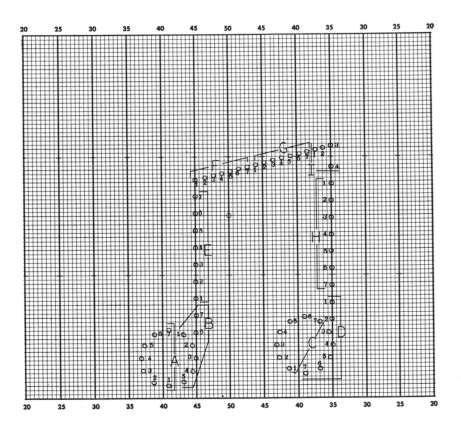

(See page xxvi for Block Band Key to Diagrams.)

Number One

Music: "I'll Walk Alone," "One Alone," "You're the Top,"
"Once in Love with Amy," "The Best of Everything,"
"One Who Really Loves You."

Action: None.

Props: None.

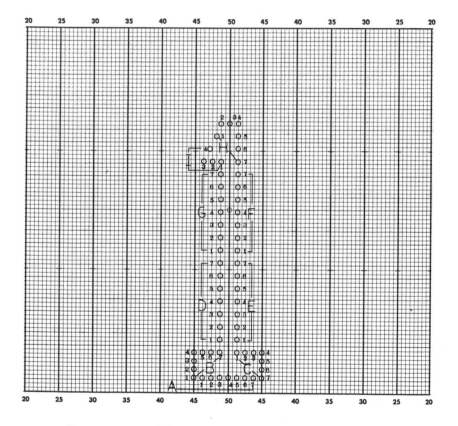

(See page xxvi for Block Band Key to Diagrams.)

117

Padlock

Music: "Steal Away," "Folsom Prison Blues," "Don't Fence Me In," "Jailhouse Rock," "Keep It a Secret," "It Is No Secret," "Prisoner of Love."

Action: None.

Props: None.

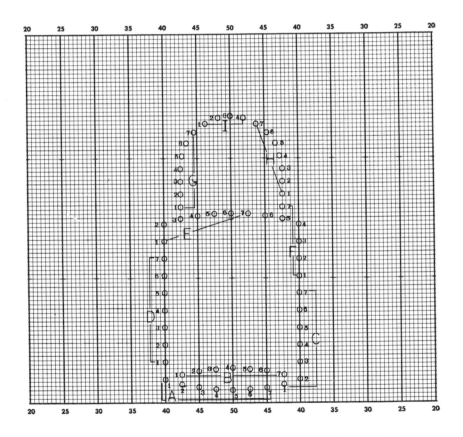

(See page xxvi for Block Band Key to Diagrams.)

Pagoda

Music: "Sukiyaka," "This Old House," "House of the Rising Sun," "Chinatown, My Chinatown."

Action: None.

Props: None.

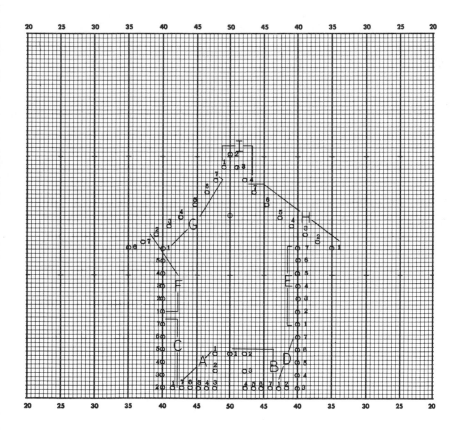

(See page xxvi for Block Band Key to Diagrams.)

Parachute

Music: "Born Free," "Falling in Love with Love," "Drifting and Dreaming," "Jumpin' at the Woodside."

Action: None.

Props: Four ropes.

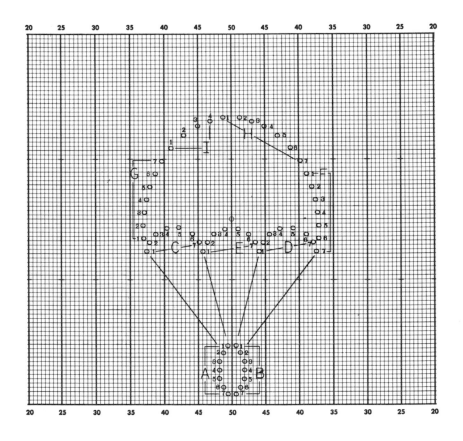

(See page xxvi for Block Band Key to Diagrams.)

Parking Meter

Music: "Five Minutes More," "Pennies from Heaven," "I Will Wait for You," "The Twist," "The Boulevard of Broken Dreams," "Turn! Turn! Turn!"

Action: Needle moves from right to left, optional.

Props: Needle.

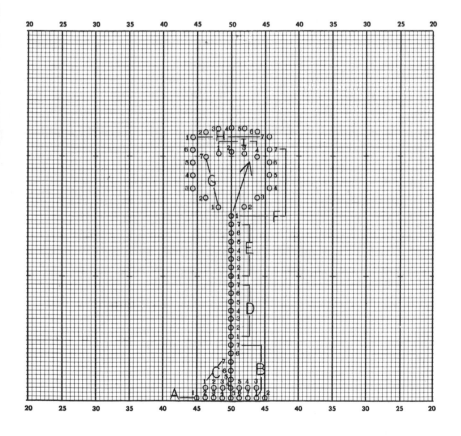

(See page xxvi for Block Band Key to Diagrams.)

P.A. System

Music: "Turkey in the Straw," "I Could Have Danced All Night," "Chicken Reel," "Dancing in the Dark."

Action: None.

Props: Two wires running from microphone to speakers.

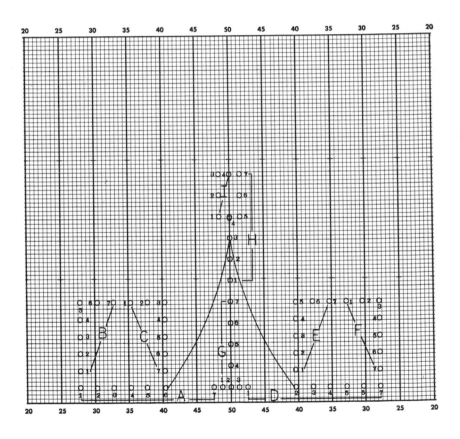

(See page xxvi for Block Band Key to Diagrams.)

Pennant

Music: Any school song, "Gaudemus Igitur," "The Halls of Ivy," "Boola Boola," "Whiffenpoof Song," "Ivory Tower."

Action: None.

Props: Appropriate letter for inside of pennant.

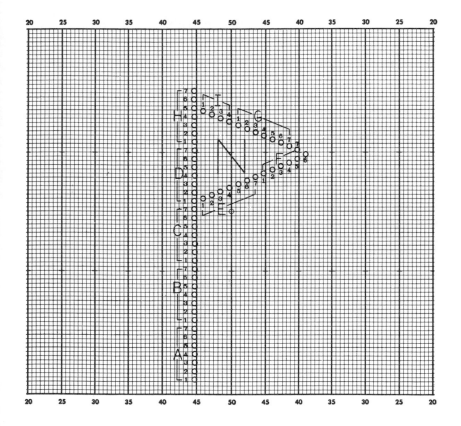

(See page xxvi for Block Band Key to Diagrams.)

Periscope

Music: "I'll Be Seeing You," "Hey Look Me Over," "I Only Have Eyes for You," "I See Your Face Before Me."

Action: None.

Props: None.

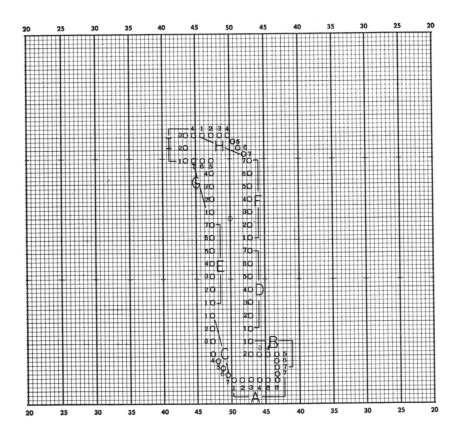

(See page xxvi for Block Band Key to Diagrams.)

Phonograph

Music: "Spinning Wheel," "The Sound of Music," "Round and Round," "I Hear a Rhapsody," "Music! Music! Music!"

Action: Wheel turns, arm moves, optional.

Props: None.

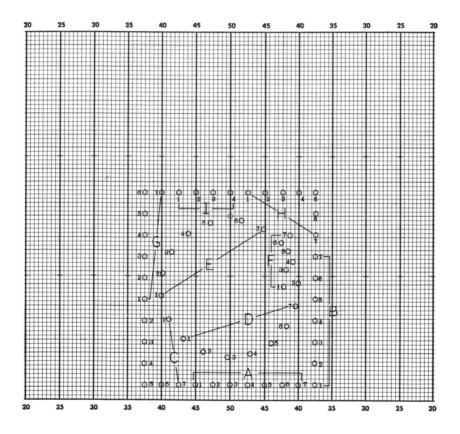

(See page xxvi for Block Band Key to Diagrams.)

125

Piano

Music: "Rhapsody in Blue," "Warsaw Concerto," "I'm Always Chasing Rainbows," "Chopsticks," Rachmaninoff's Concerto.

Action: None.

Props: None.

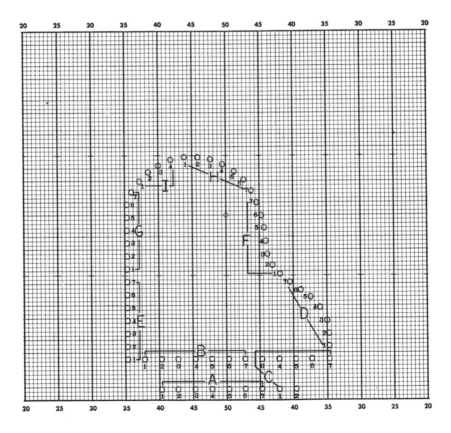

(See page xxvi for Block Band Key to Diagrams.)

Pick

Music: "Sixteen Tons," "Big Bad John," "Dig You Later,"
"Golden Earrings," "Climb Every Mountain," "I've
Been Working on the Railroad."

Action: None.

Props: None.

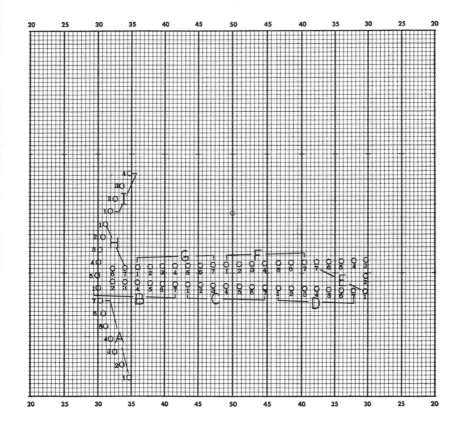

(See page xxvi for Block Band Key to Diagrams.)

Pinball Machine

Music: "Mr. Lucky," "Games People Play," "It's All in the Game," "Taking a Chance on Love," "Game of Love."

Action: Plunger moves left and right, optional.

Props: None.

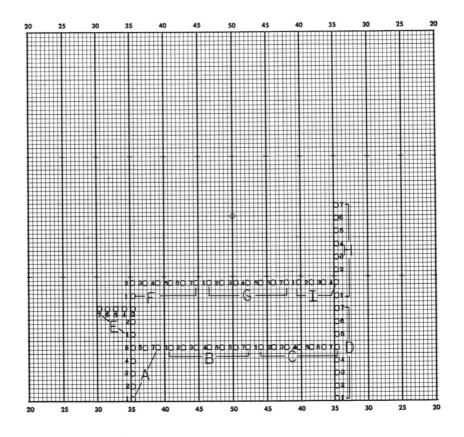

(See page xxvi for Block Band Key to Diagrams.)

Pipe

Music: "Smoke Gets in Your Eyes," "On Top of Old Smoky," "Light My Fire," "Fire," "Ritual Fire Dance."

Action: Smoke trails upward, optional.

Props: None.

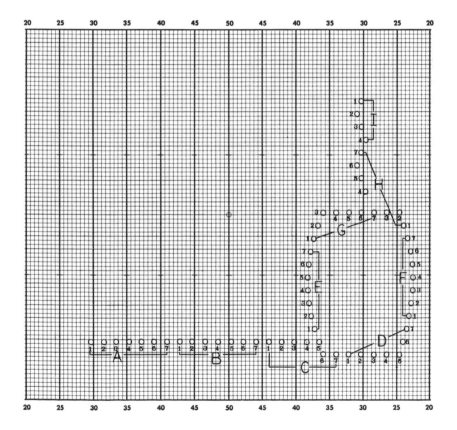

(See page xxvi for Block Band Key to Diagrams.)

Pitchfork

Music: "Old Devil Moon," "The Farmer in the Dell," "Heat Wave," "Hot Diggity," "A Hot Time in the Old Town," "Ritual Fire Dance."

Action: None.

Props: None.

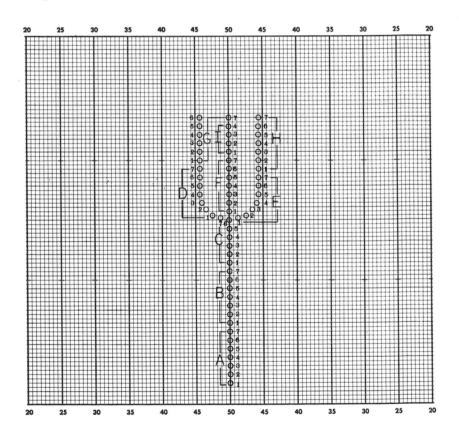

(See page xxvi for Block Band Key to Diagrams.)

Pumpkin

Music: "That Old Black Magic," "Put on a Happy Face,"
         "Black Magic Woman," "Bewitched," "Make Believe."

Action: None.

Props: Eyes and nose, mouth.

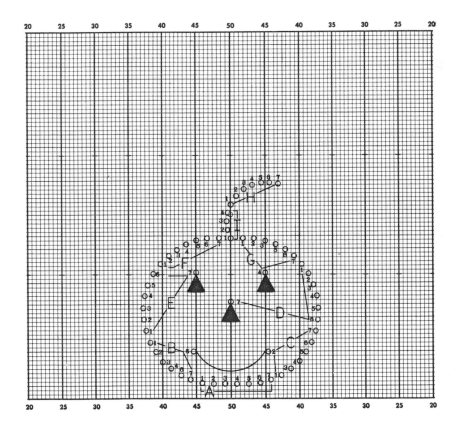

(See page xxvi for Block Band Key to Diagrams.)

Pyramids

Music: "Swingin' Safari," "Caravan," "The Desert Song," "The Sheik of Araby," "Cool, Cool Water."

Action: None.

Props: None.

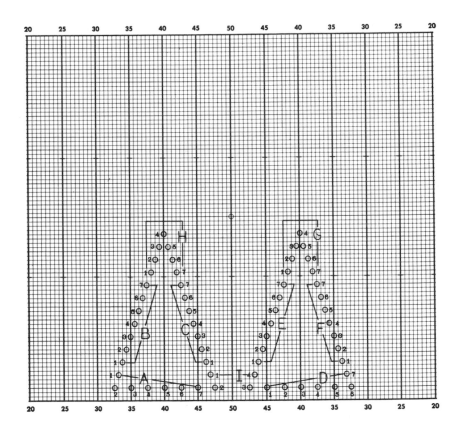

(See page xxvi for Block Band Key to Diagrams.)

Question Mark

Music: "What Now My Love," "Whatever Lola Wants," "Who?" "Why Don't You Believe Me?" "How Do You Speak to an Angel?"

Action: None.

Props: None.

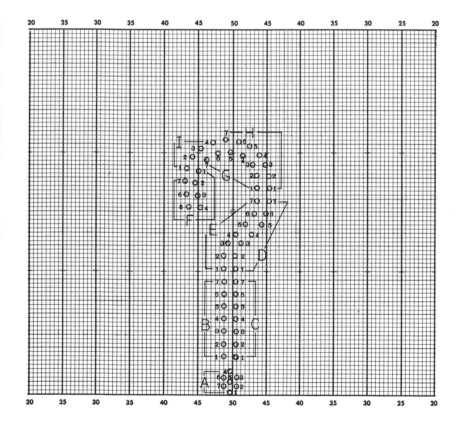

(See page xxvi for Block Band Key to Diagrams.)

Rainbow

Music: "Over the Rainbow," "I'm Always Chasing Rainbows," "The Day the Rains Came," "Don't Let the Rain Come Down."

Action: None.

Props: None.

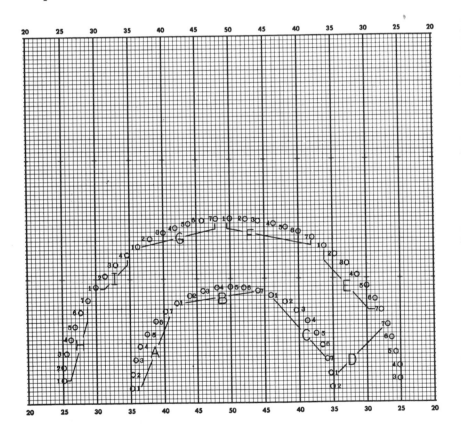

(See page xxvi for Block Band Key to Diagrams.)

Rickshaw

Music: "Chinatown, My Chinatown," "Japanese Sandman," "Sukiyaka," "Chopsticks," "The House of the Rising Sun," "On a Slow Boat to China."

Action: Wheel rotates, optional.

Props: Wheel spokes, optional.

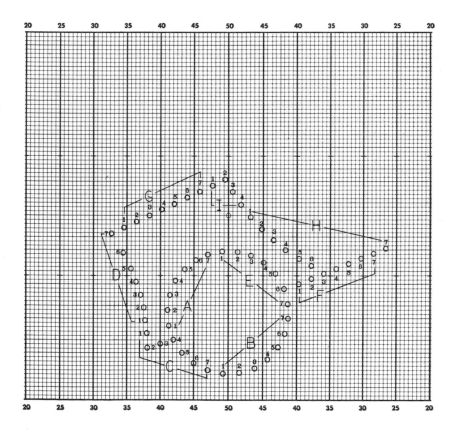

(See page xxvi for Block Band Key to Diagrams.)

Rifle

Music: "How the West Was Won," "Peter Gunn," "Feudin'
and Fightin'," "I'm Shooting High," "I Get a Kick Out
of You," "Gunsmoke."

Action: None.

Props: None.

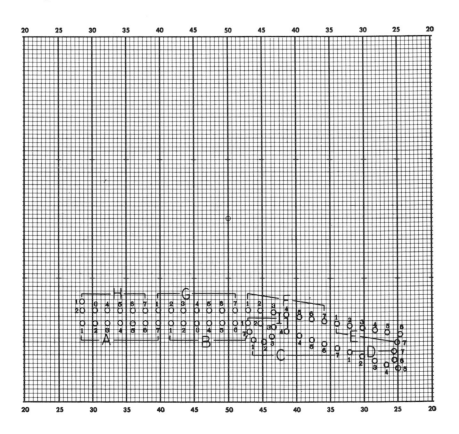

(See page xxvi for Block Band Key to Diagrams.)

Ring or Wheel

Music: "Wedding March," "Love and Marriage," "The Girl That I Marry," "Round and Round," "Wheel of Fortune," "Spinning Wheel."

Action: Ring rotates, optional.

Props: None.

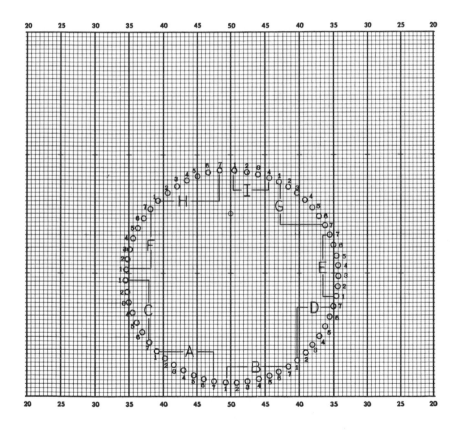

(See page xxvi for Block Band Key to Diagrams.)

River Boat

Music: "Cruising Down the River," "Ol' Man River," "Ebb Tide," "Cry Me a River," "Waiting for the Robert E. Lee."

Action: Paddle wheel rotates, optional.

Props: None.

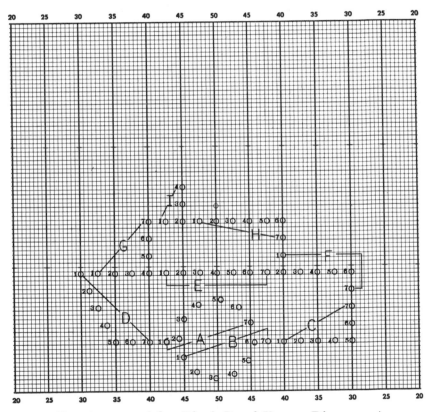

(See page xxvi for Block Band Key to Diagrams.)

Rolling Pin

Music: "Sweet Lorraine," "You Always Hurt the One You Love," "Mama Inez," "Yes Sir, That's My Baby," "Bill Bailey, Won't You Please Come Home?" "You Go to My Head," "Whatever Lola Wants."

Action: None.

Props: None.

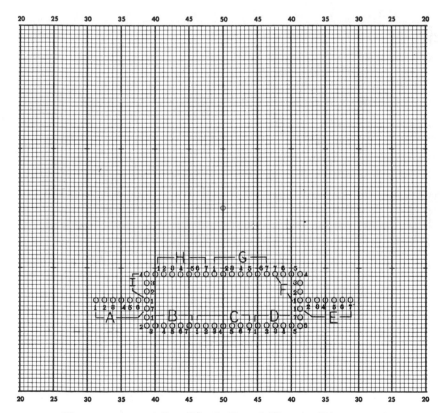

(See page xxvi for Block Band Key to Diagrams.)

Sailboat

Music: "Windy," "Born Free," "Sail Along, Silvery Moon,"
"Where the Boys Are," "Red Sails in the Sunset,"
"Cast Your Fate to the Wind."

Action: None.

Props: Two ropes, optional.

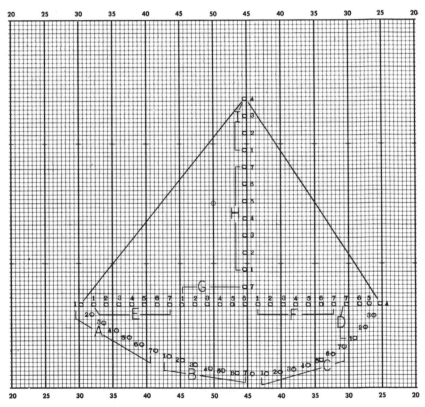

(See page xxvi for Block Band Key to Diagrams.)

Scales

Music: "How Great Thou Art," "Little Things Mean a Lot,"
"Big Bad John," "Too Fat Polka," "Candy Kisses,"
"Sixteen Tons," "My Heart Tells Me," "Anchors
Aweigh."

Action: Needle moves, optional.

Props: Needle, optional.

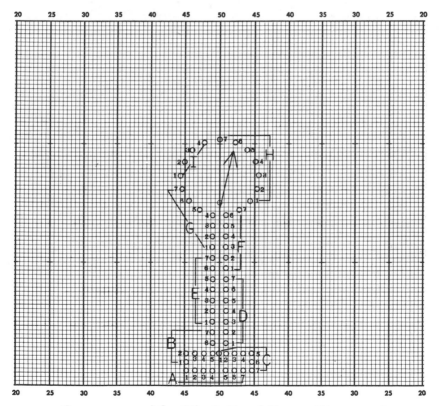

(See page xxvi for Block Band Key to Diagrams.)

141

Sharp, Flat, Natural Signs

Music: "Gillette Look Sharp March," "The Flat Foot Floogee," "Doin' What Comes Natur'lly," "Strike Up the Band."

Action: None.

Props: None.

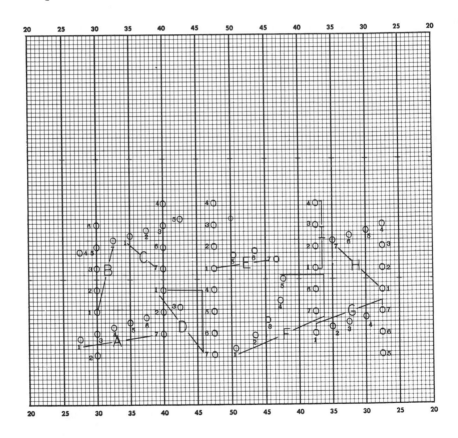

(See page xxvi for Block Band Key to Diagrams.)

Ship

Music: *Victory at Sea*, "Ebb Tide," "Over the Waves," "Windy," "Cruising Down the River," "Red Sails in the Sunset."

Action: None.

Props: None.

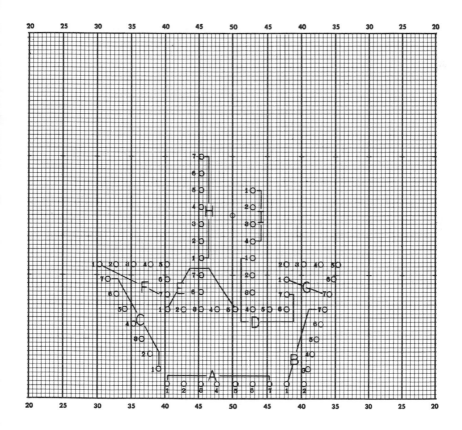

(See page xxvi for Block Band Key to Diagrams.)

Shortwave Radio

Music: "Far Away Places," "I Hear a Rhapsody," "Over the Waves," "So Far Away," "Close to You," "Peter Gunn."

Action: None.

Props: None.

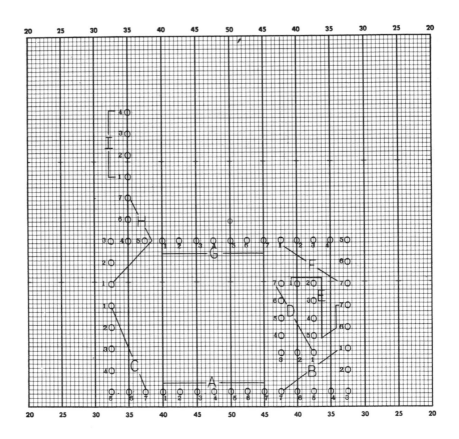

(See page xxvi for Block Band Key to Diagrams.)

Sign, traffic

Music: "Bus Stop," "Stop! In the Name of Love," "Slow-poke," "I Will Wait for You," "Wait 'til the Sun Shines, Nellie," "Goin' Out of My Head."

Action: None.

Props: Sign in middle of formation.

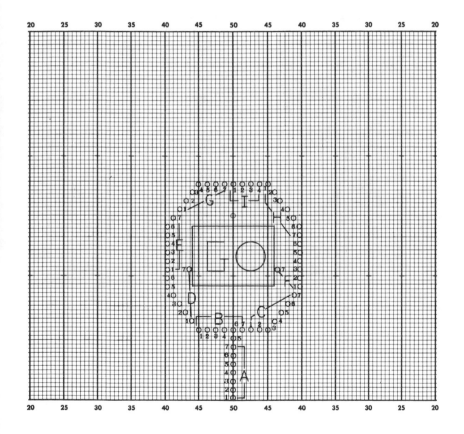

(See page xxvi for Block Band Key to Diagrams.)

145

Skyline

Music: "Downtown," "Manhattan Serenade," "Look for the Silver Lining," "A Foggy Day," "Misty," "Smoke Gets in Your Eyes," "Chicago."

Action: None.

Props: None.

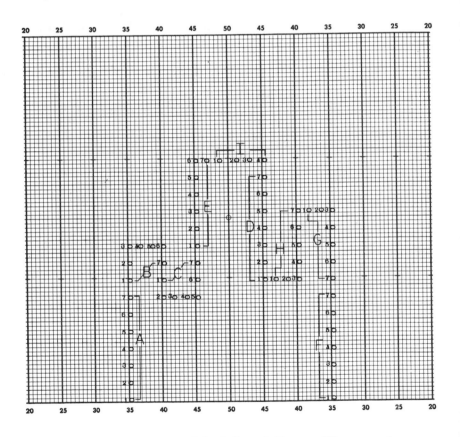

(See page xxvi for Block Band Key to Diagrams.)

Sled

Music: "Sleigh Ride," "Snowbird," "Slipping Around," "Let It Snow! Let It Snow! Let It Snow!"

Action: Formation moves to right, optional.

Props: None.

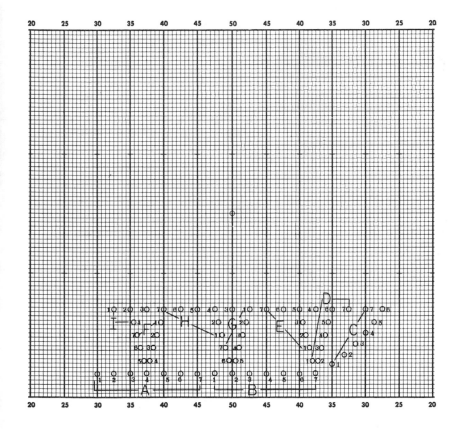

(See page xxvi for Block Band Key to Diagrams.)

147

Sleep Sounds

Music: "Sleepy Time Gal," "Lazy Bones," "Dream," "Sleep," "The Impossible Dream," "When It's Sleepy Time Down South," "Drifting and Dreaming."

Action: None.

Props: None.

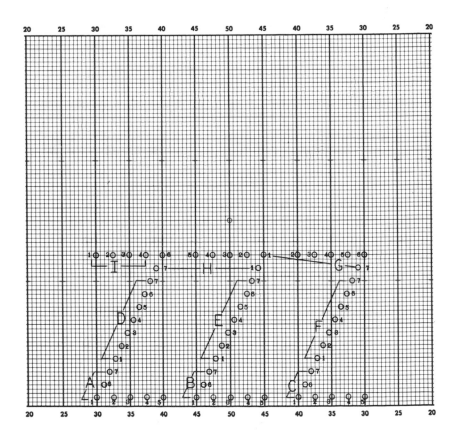

(See page xxvi for Block Band Key to Diagrams.)

Snake

Music: "Shake, Rattle and Roll," "Walk on by," "Song of India," "Hey, Look Me Over," "Bewitched."

Action: Tongue moves, optional.

Props: None.

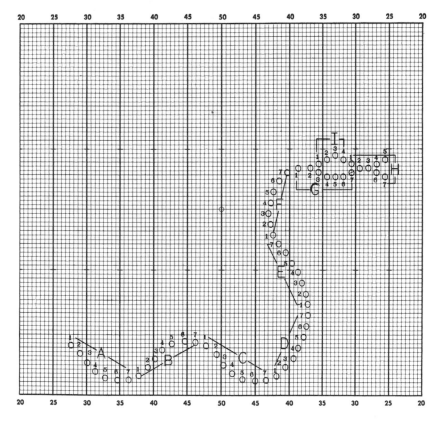

(See page xxvi for Block Band Key to Diagrams.)

Snake and Basket

Music: "Song of India," "Indian Love Call," "Blowin' in the Wind," "Calcutta."

Action: Snake moves, optional.

Props: None.

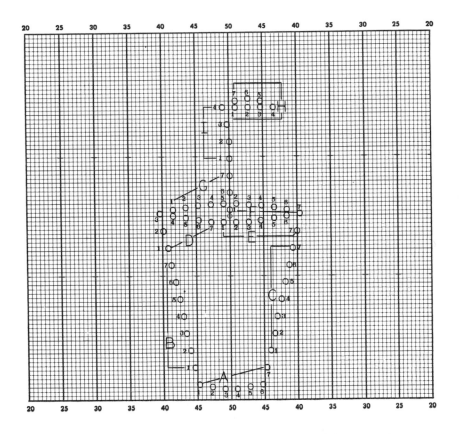

(See page xxvi for Block Band Key to Diagrams.)

Snowman

Music: "Frosty the Snowman," "Snowbird," "Winter Wonderland," "Cold, Cold Heart," "Let It Snow! Let It Snow! Let It Snow!"

Action: None.

Props: None.

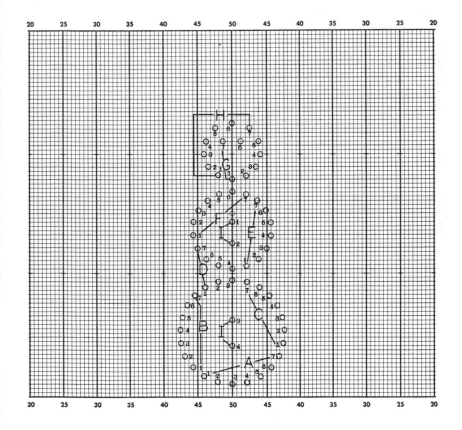

(See page xxvi for Block Band Key to Diagrams.)

151

Soldier

Music: "Parade of the Wooden Soldiers," "The Ballad of the Green Berets," "Marine's Hymn," "The Caisson Song," "Sound Off," "March of the Little Leaden Soldiers."

Action: Body parts move, optional.

Props: None.

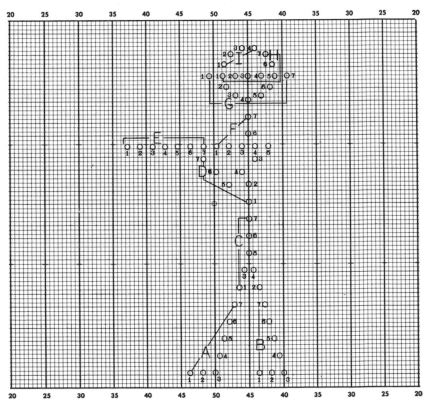

(See page xxvi for Block Band Key to Diagrams.)

Sombrero

Music: "Spanish Eyes," "Lady of Spain," "The Lonely Bull," "In a Little Spanish Town," "Adios," "April in Portugal."

Action: None.

Props: None.

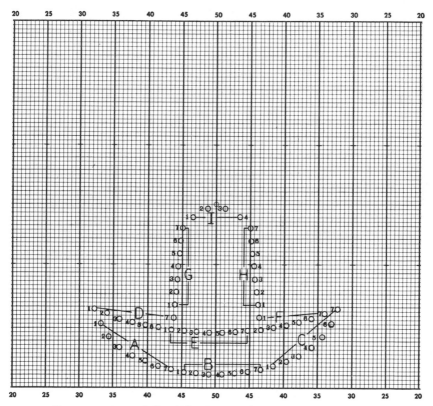

(See page xxvi for Block Band Key to Diagrams.)

153

Spanish Mission

Music: "Vaya Con Dios," "The Three Bells," "South of the Border," "Ave Maria," "The Impossible Dream."

Action: None.

Props: None.

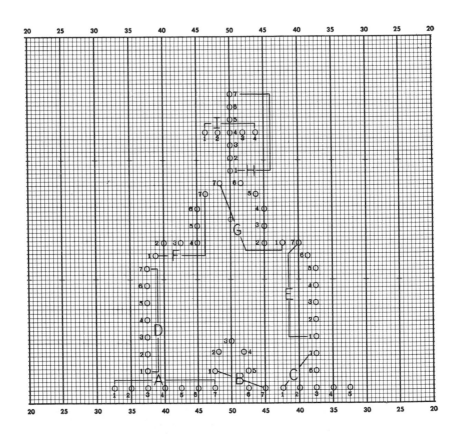

(See page xxvi for Block Band Key to Diagrams.)

Spear

Music: "Swingin' Safari," "Tiger Rag," "Pink Panther," "On the Trail," "Black Magic Woman," "You Always Hurt the One You Love."

Action: Arrow moves to right, optional.

Props: None.

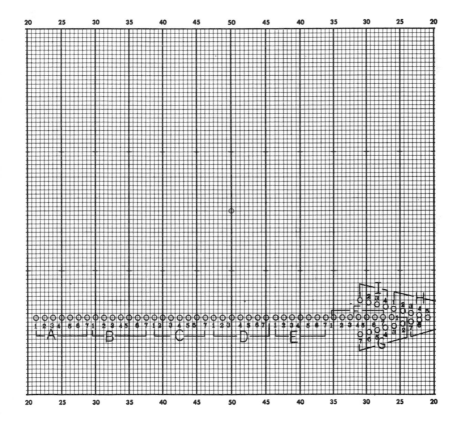

(See page xxvi for Block Band Key to Diagrams.)

155

Stage

Music: "Lullaby of Broadway," "The Stripper," "Make Be- lieve," "Strike Up the Band," "There's No Business Like Show Business."

Action: Curtains close or open, optional.

Props: None.

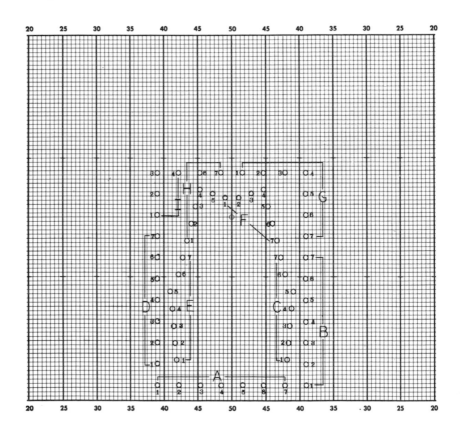

(See page xxvi for Block Band Key to Diagrams.)

Stairs

Music: "Stairway to the Stars," "Climb Every Mountain," "Up Tight," "Heartaches," "Up, Up and Away."

Action: None.

Props: None.

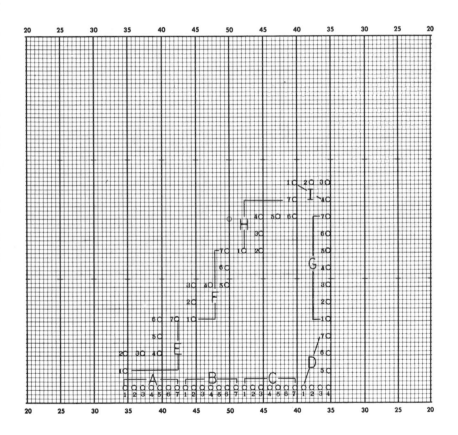

(See page xxvi for Block Band Key to Diagrams.)

157

Star

Music: "Superstar," "Star Dust," "When You Wish Upon a Star," "You Are My Lucky Star," "Stars in My Eyes," "Starbright."

Action: None.

Props: None.

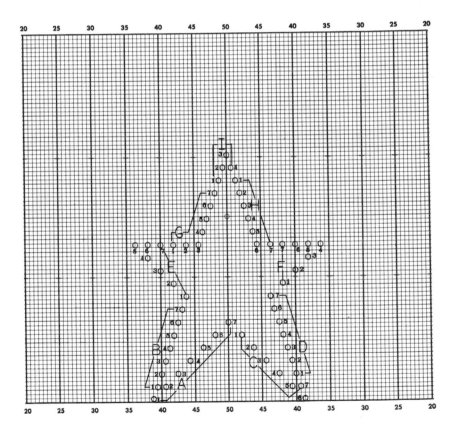

(See page xxvi for Block Band Key to Diagrams.)

Stereo, cassette

Music: "The Sound of Music," "Sounds of Silence," "Music to Watch Girls By," "Music! Music! Music!," "Play a Simple Melody."

Action: None.

Props: Two connecting wires from deck to speakers.

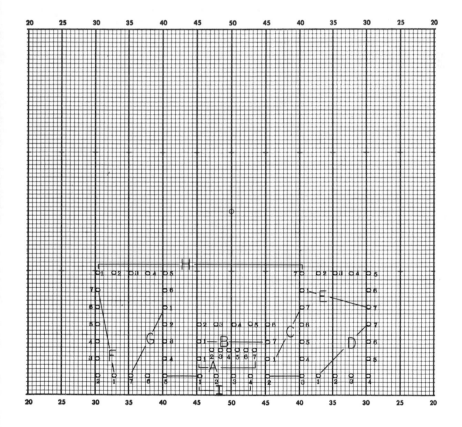

(See page xxvi for Block Band Key to Diagrams.)

Street Light

Music: "Night and Day," "The Lamp Is Low," "Standing on the Corner," "Lamplighter's Serenade," "Strangers in the Night."

Action: None.

Props: None.

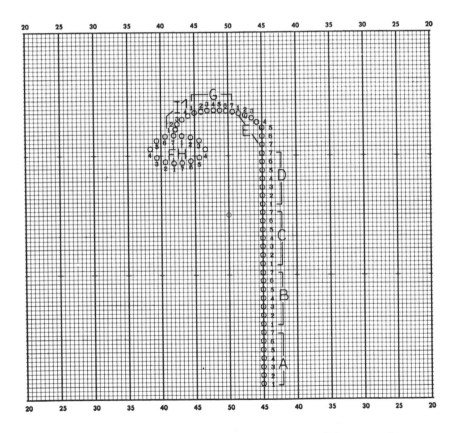

(See page xxvi for Block Band Key to Diagrams.)

Street Sign

Music: "Slaughter on Tenth Avenue," "Standing on the Corner," "On the Street Where You Live," "Lullaby of Broadway."

Action: None.

Props: Sign information.

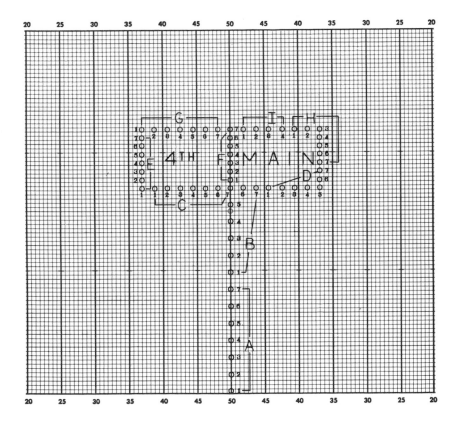

(See page xxvi for Block Band Key to Diagrams.)

Stripes

Music: "Marine's Hymn," "Caisson Song," "Air Force Song," "Anchor's Aweigh," "Feudin' and Fightin'," "This Is My Country."

Action: None.

Props: None.

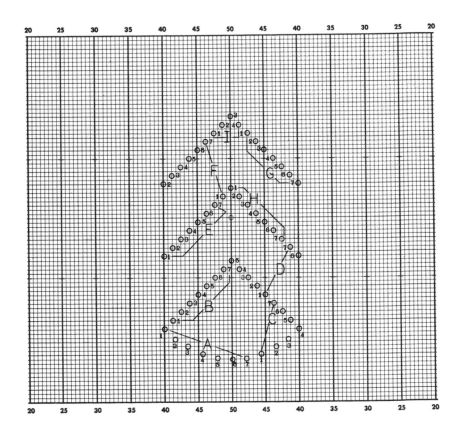

(See page xxvi for Block Band Key to Diagrams.)

Submarine

Music: *Victory at Sea,* "Sink the Bismark," "How Deep Is the Ocean," "Asleep in the Deep," "Deep River."

Action: Formation goes right, left or up, optional.

Props: None.

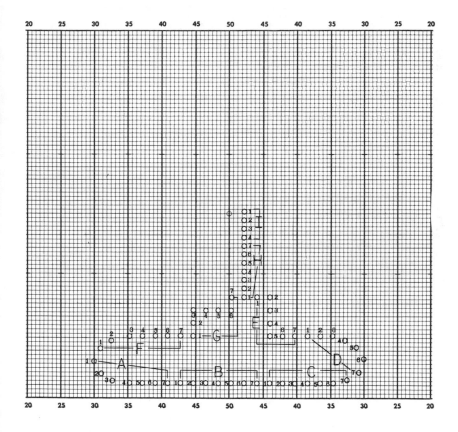

(See page xxvi for Block Band Key to Diagrams.)

Sun

Music: "Sunny," "Blue Skies," "Canadian Sunset," "Summer-time," "Heat Wave," "That Lucky Old Sun," "When You're Hot, You're Hot."

Action: None.

Props: None.

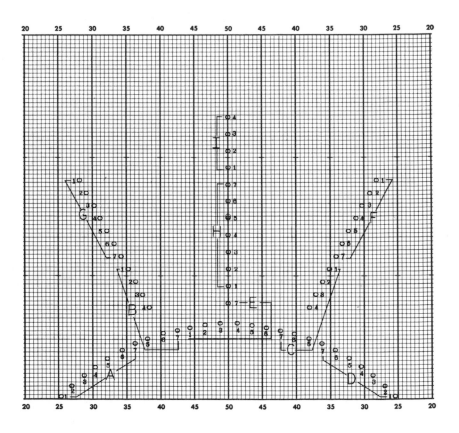

(See page xxvi for Block Band Key to Diagrams.)

Swing

Music: "Swinging on a Star," "Swingin' Safari," "Back in Your Own Back Yard," "Swingin' Shepherd Blues."

Action: None.

Props: None.

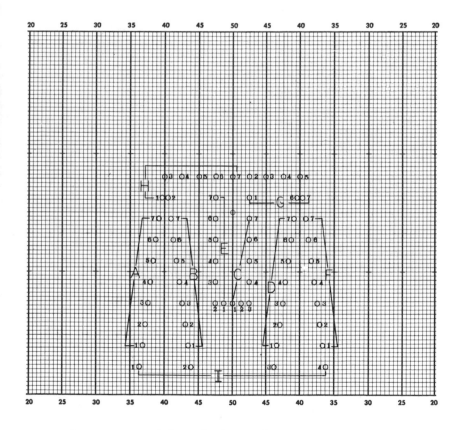

(See page xxvi for Block Band Key to Diagrams.)

165

Sword

Music: "Mack the Knife," "Sabre Dance," "You Always Hurt
the One You Love," "Tenderly," "Swingin' Safari."

Action: None.

Props: None.

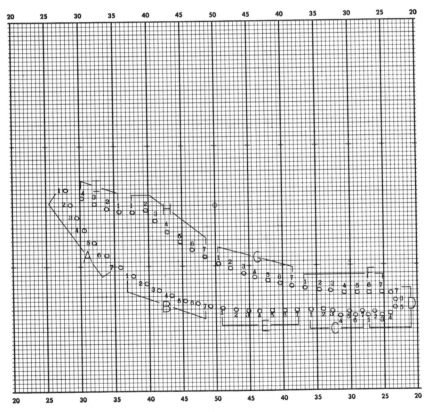

(See page xxvi for Block Band Key to Diagrams.)

Table

Music: "Days of Wine and Roses," "Tea for Two," "Let's Have Another Cup o' Coffee," "Dinner at Eight," "Sing for Your Supper," "You Turned the Tables on Me."

Action: None.

Props: None.

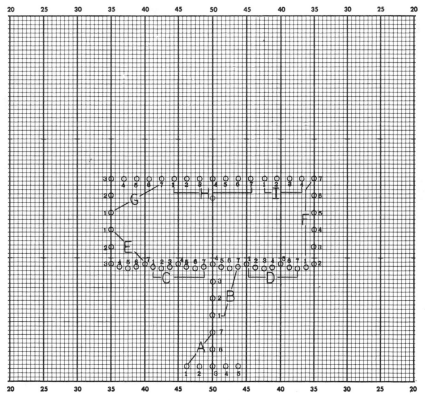

(See page xxvi for Block Bank Key to Diagrams.)

Tank

Music: "Feudin' and Fightin'," "America," "The Desert Song," "This Is the Army, Mr. Jones," "Song of the Open Road."

Action: Gun raises or lowers, turret turns, track rotates, optional.

Props: Gun.

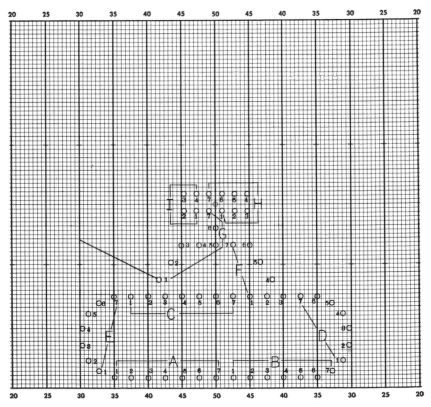

(See page xxvi for Block Band Key to Diagrams.)

Teeter-totter

Music: "School Days, School Days," "Undecided," "I'm Sitting on Top of the World," "Falling in Love with Love," "Up, Up and Away."

Action: Board teeters, optional.

Props: None.

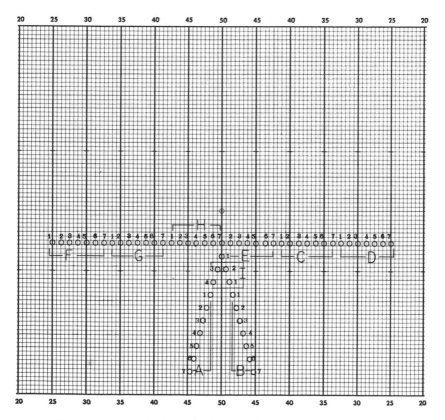

(See page xxvi for Block Band Key to Diagrams.)

Telephone

Music: "Speak Low," "Call Me Irresponsible," "PA 6500," "Wichita Lineman," "Bells Are Ringing," "Let Me Call You Sweetheart."

Action: None.

Props: Circular dial.

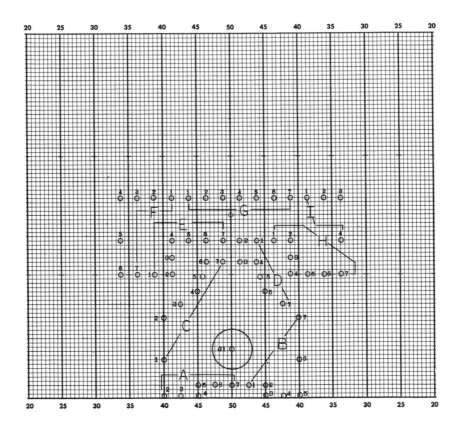

(See page xxvi for Block Band Key to Diagrams.)

Telescope

Music: "I'll Be Seeing You," "Hey, Look Me Over," "Look of Love," "Star Dust," "Moonglow," "Stars in My Eyes."

Action: Eye piece moves in and out, optional.

Props: None.

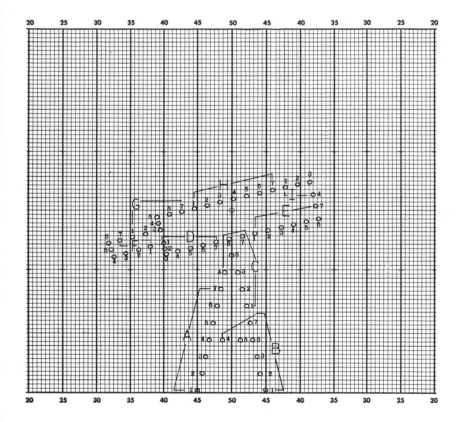

(See page xxvi for Block Band Key to Diagrams.)

Tent, circus

Music: "Entry of the Gladiators," "Barnum and Bailey's Favorite," "The Big Cage," "Baby Elephant Walk," "The Pink Panther," "Tiger Rag," "See You Later, Alligator."

Action: None.

Props: Flag twirlers on high points, as banners, optional.

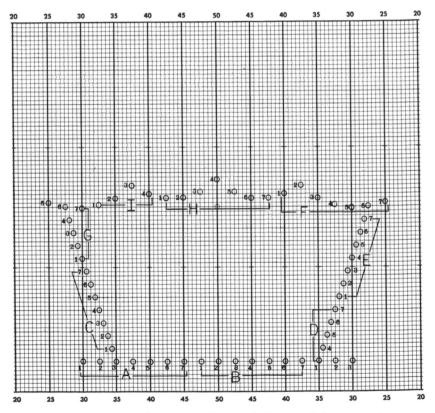

(See page xxvi for Block Band Key to Diagrams.)

172

Tent, pup

Music: "You're in the Army Now," "Tenting Tonight," "Under a Blanket of Blue," "This Is the Army, Mr. Jones."

Action: None.

Props: None.

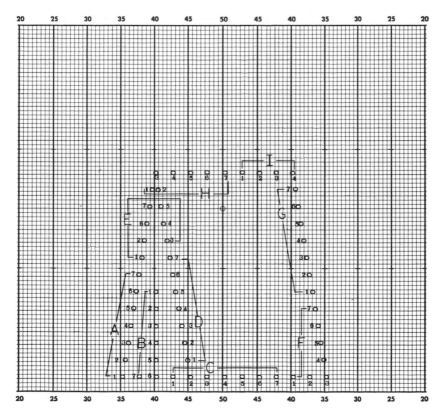

(See page xxvi for Block Band Key to Diagrams.)

Thermometer

Music: "Five Foot Two," "One Dozen Roses," "Route 66," "Seventy-six Trombones."

Action: Mercury rises to numbers, in order.

Props: Mercury (paper streamer plus cardboard circle), numbers.

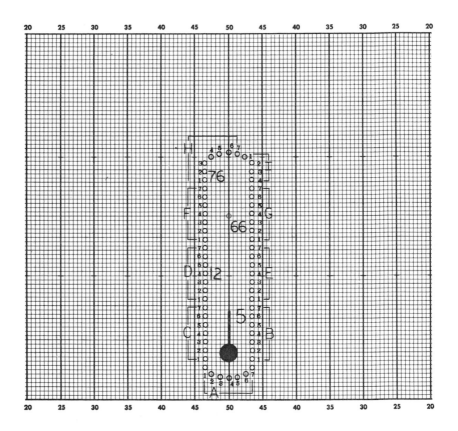

(See page xxvi for Block Band Key to Diagrams.)

Tic-Tac-Toe

Music: "Games People Play," "Takes Two to Tango," "School Days," "It's All in the Game," "Your Cheatin' Heart."

Action: None.

Props: None.

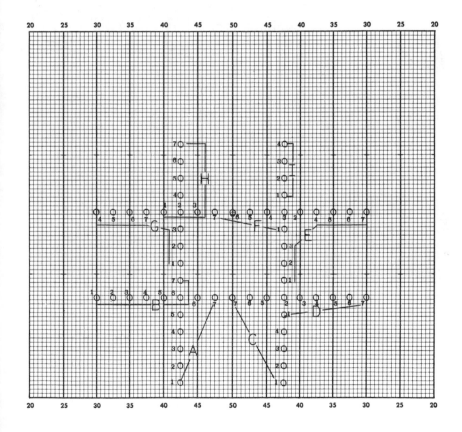

(See page xxvi for Block Band Key to Diagrams.)

Tightrope

Music: "I'll Walk the Line," "Cotton Candy," "I'll Walk Alone," "The Peanut Vendor."

Action: None.

Props: None.

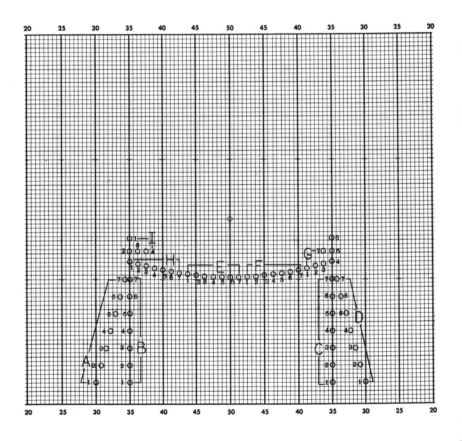

(See page xxvi for Block Band Key to Diagrams.)

Tomahawk

Music: "Indian Reservation," "Cherokee," "Ten Little Indians," "You Go to My Head," "Indian Love Call."

Action: None.

Props: None.

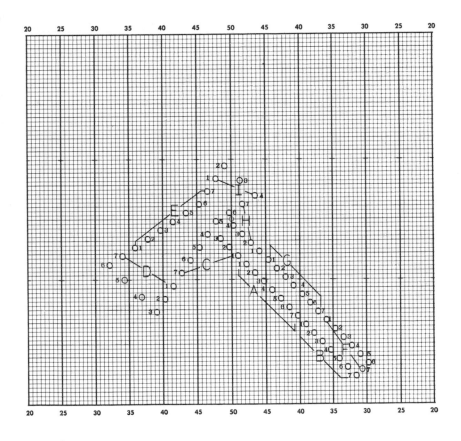

(See page xxvi for Block Band Key to Diagrams.)

Tote Bag

Music: "Put on a Happy Face," "Make Believe," "Reflec-
tions," "Look for the Silver Lining."

Action: None.

Props: None.

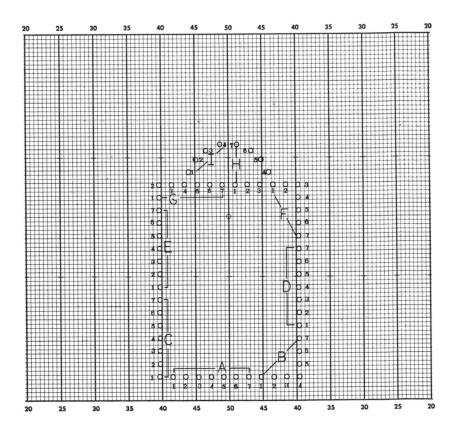

(See page xxvi for Block Band Key to Diagrams.)

Tractor

Music: "Old MacDonald Had a Farm," "The Farmer in the Dell," "Summertime," "In the Good Old Summer Time."

Action: Wheels rotate, optional.

Props: Wheels spokes, optional.

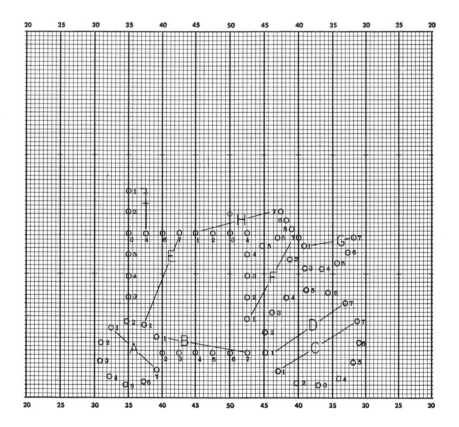

(See page xxvi for Block Band Key to Diagrams.)

179

Train

Music: "This Train," "Night Train," "Casey Jones," "Take the 'A' Train," "Chattanooga Choo-Choo."

Action: Wheels rotate, optional.

Props: None.

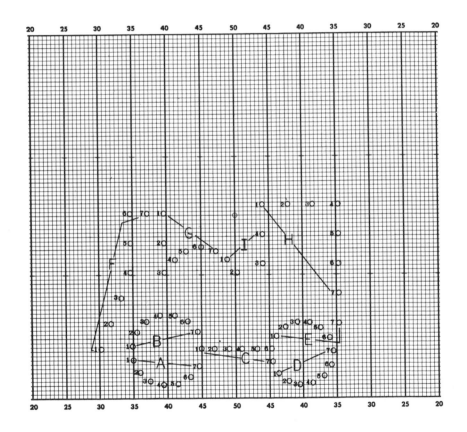

(See page xxvi for Block Band Key to Diagrams.)

Tree, Christmas or pine

Music: "The Tree in the Meadow," "Trees," "Sparrow in the Tree Top," "The Trail of the Lonesome Pine."

Action: None.

Props: None.

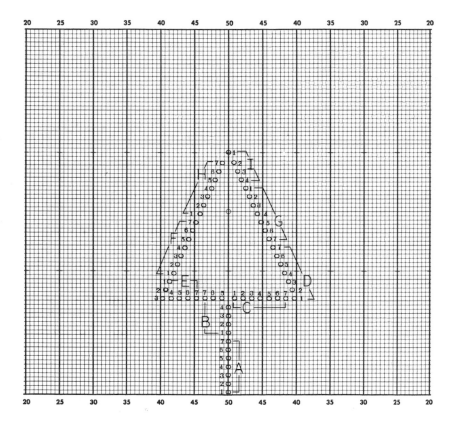

(See page xxvi for Block Band Key to Diagrams.)

Tree, palm

Music: "Hawaiian Wedding Song," "Hawaii Five-O," "Bali Hai," "On the Good Ship Lollipop," "Aloha Oe," "Hawaiian War Chant."

Action: Branches wave in breeze, optional.

Props: None.

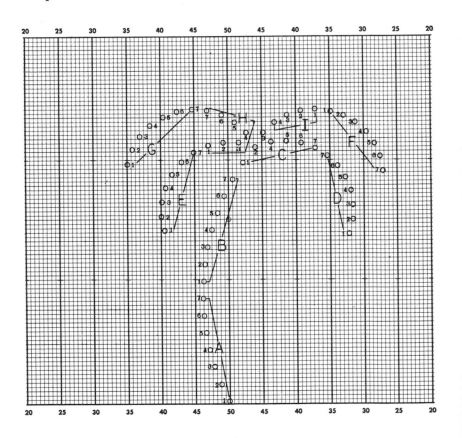

(See page xxvi for Block Band Key to Diagrams.)

Tree, shade

Music: "Autumn Leaves," "Don't Sit Under the Apple Tree," "Apple Blossom Time," "Naughty Lady of Shady Lane," "Autumn Serenade."

Action: None.

Props: None.

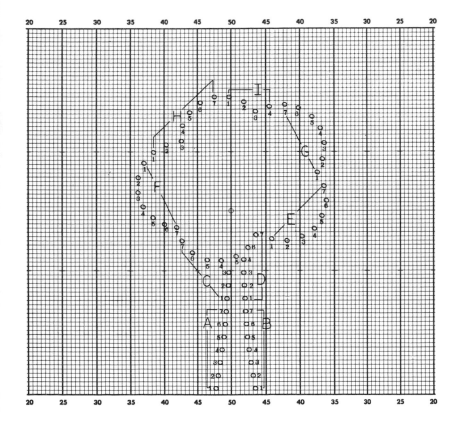

(See page xxvi for Block Band Key to Diagrams.)

183

Trombone

Music: "Seventy-six Trombones," "Lassus Trombone," "Slipping Around," "Holiday for Trombones."

Action: Slide moves in and out, optional.

Props: None.

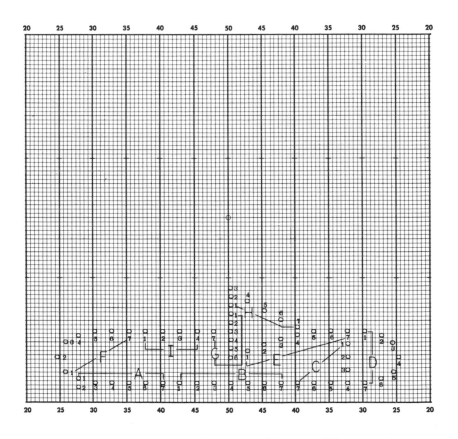

(See page xxvi for Block Band Key to Diagrams.)

Turtle

Music: "Slowpoke," "Sixteen Tons," "Take It Easy," "Talk to the Animals," "This Ole House," "The House of the Rising Sun."

Action: Head and tail move, optional.

Props: None.

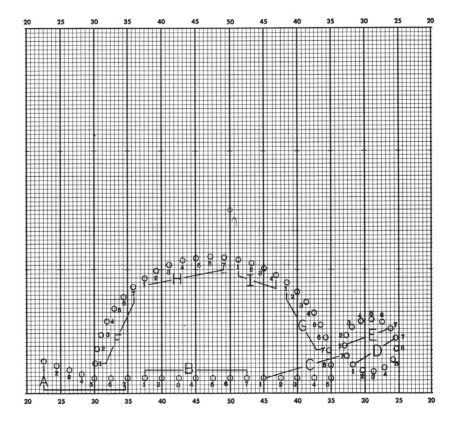

(See page xxvi for Block Band Key to Diagrams.)

Umbrella, beach

Music: "Sunny," "Ebb Tide," "Summertime," "By the Beautiful Sea," "Surfin' Safari," "Where the Boys Are."

Action: None.

Props: None.

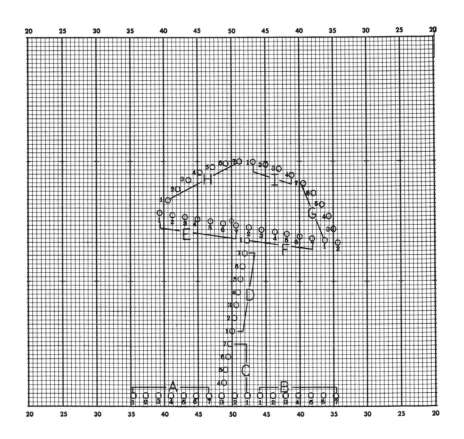

(See page xxvi for Block Band Key to Diagrams.)

Umbrella, rain

Music: "Singin' in the Rain," "Raindrops," "Raindrops Keep Falling On My Head," "The Day the Rains Came," "The Rain in Spain."

Action: Umbrella folds down, optional.

Props: None.

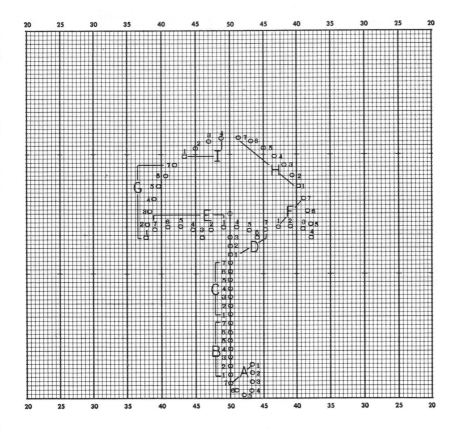

(See page xxvi for Block Band Key to Diagrams.)

Umbrella Table

Music: "Come Rain or Come Shine," "Sunny," "Picnic," "Summertime."

Action: None.

Props: None.

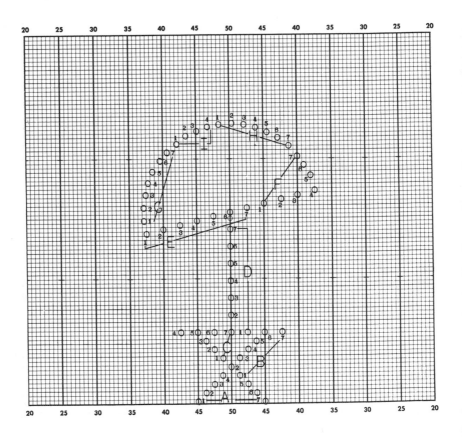

(See page xxvi for Block Band Key to Diagrams.)

Victory (Peace) Sign

Music: "Victor's March," *Victory at Sea*, "Peaceful Valley," "Liberty Bell March."

Action: None.

Props: None.

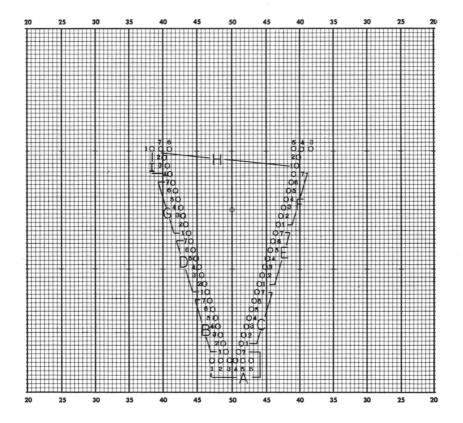

(See page xxvi for Block Band Key to Diagrams.)

Wagon, covered

Music: "Wagon Wheels," "On the Trail," "How the West Was Won," "Mule Train," "California Here I Come."

Action: Wheels rotate, optional.

Props: Wheel spokes, optional.

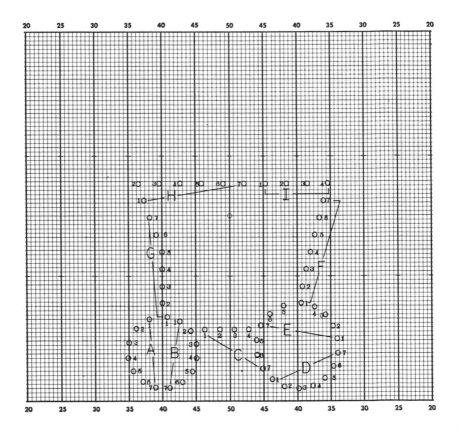

(See page xxvi for Block Band Key to Diagrams.)

Walkie-Talkies

Music: "Side by Side," "How Do You Speak to an Angel?"
         "Speak Low," "Talk to the Animals," "Hello, Dolly!"

Action: None.

Props: None.

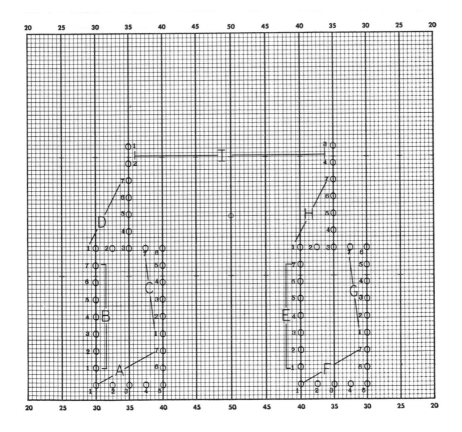

(See page xxvi for Block Band Key to Diagrams.)

Washington Monument

Music: "Washington Post," "Yankee Doodle," "This Is My Country," "God Bless America," "Washington and Lee Swing."

Action: None.

Props: None.

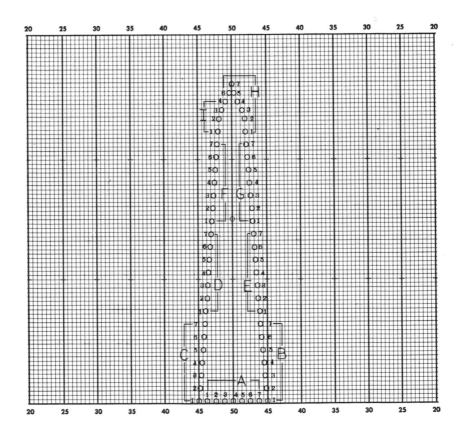

(See page xxvi for Block Band Key to Diagrams.)

Water Tower

Music: "Downtown," "Waterloo," "Drinking Song," "Dry Bones," "Drink to Me Only with Thine Eyes."

Action: None.

Props: None.

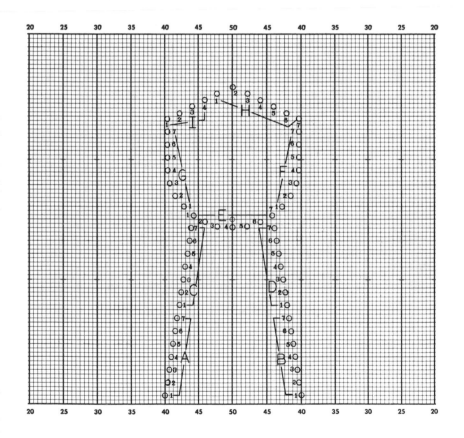

(See page xxvi for Block Band Key to Diagrams.)

Wedding Rings

Music: "Wedding March," "Anniversary Song," "Anniversary Waltz," "Bells Are Ringing," "I Kiss Your Hand, Madame."

Action: None.

Props: None.

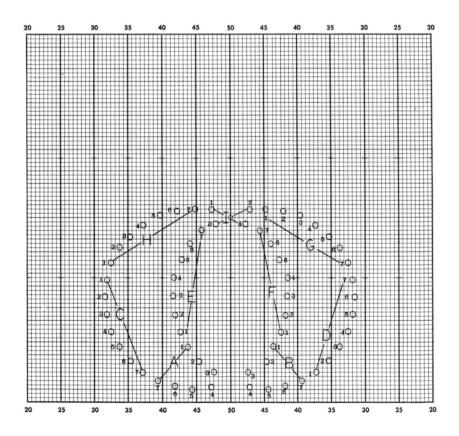

(See page xxvi for Block Band Key to Diagrams.)

Wheelbarrow

Music: "Whistle While You Work," "I've Been Working on the Railroad," "Sixteen Tons," "Big Bad John."

Action: Wheel rotates, optional.

Props: None.

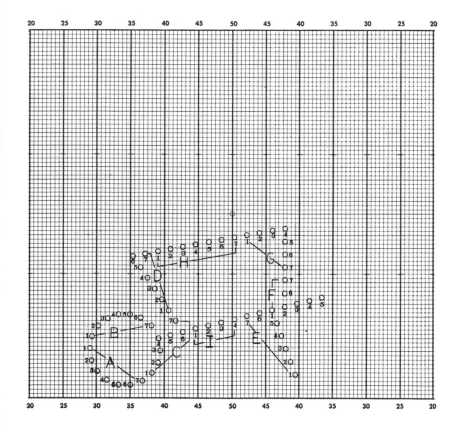

(See page xxvi for Block Band Key to Diagrams.)

Whistle

Music: "Dragnet," "Peter Gunn," "Whistle While You Work," "Strike Up the Band," "March of the Little Leaden Soldiers."

Action: None.

Props: None.

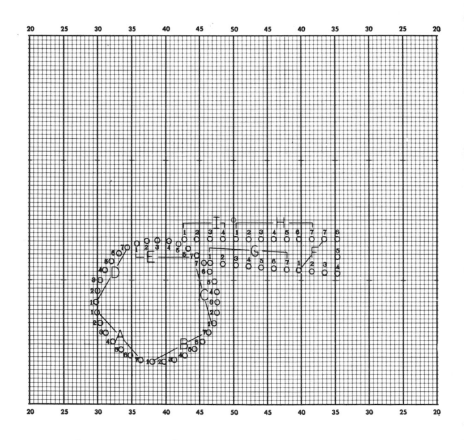

(See page xxvi for Block Band Key to Diagrams.)

Wigwam

Music: "Indian Love Call," "Cherokee," "Indian Summer," "Ten Little Indians."

Action: None.

Props: None.

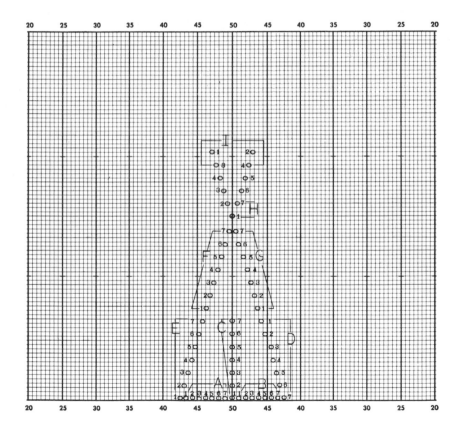

(See page xxvi for Block Band Key to Diagrams.)

197

Wind Chimes

Music: "Windy," "The Breeze and I," "The Sound of Music," "Sounds of Silence," "I Hear a Rhapsody."

Action: Chimes move, optional.

Props: None.

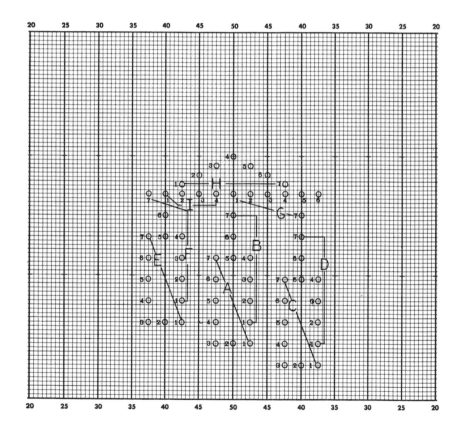

(See page xxvi for Block Band Key to Diagrams.)

Windmill

Music: "Windmills of Your Mind," "Windy," "The Breeze and I," "In an Old Dutch Garden."

Action: Arms rotate, optional.

Props: None.

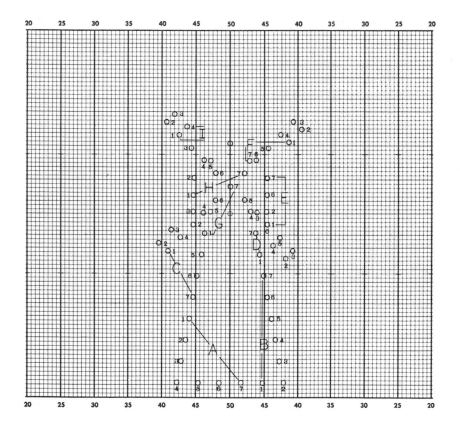

(See page xxvi for Block Band Key to Diagrams.)

Wishing Well

Music: "When You Wish Upon a Star," "Wish You Were Here," "I Wish You Love," "I Wish I Didn't Love You So," "Dream."

Action: None.

Props: None.

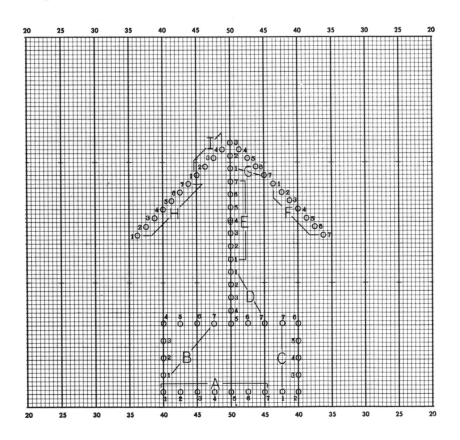

(See page xxvi for Block Band Key to Diagrams.)

Musical Selection Finder

Titles:	Formations and Pages:
Adios	Sombrero 153
A Fool Such as I	Cap, dunce 37
Air Force Song	Airplane 1, stripes 162
Alabamy Bound	Cap, Confederate 36
Alley Cat	Cat 43
Alley Oop	Dinosaur 63
All of Me	Bomb 21
All Shook Up	Bottle, chemistry 24
Aloha Oe	Tree, palm 182
Amen	Cross 58
America	Flag 79, tank 168
American in Paris, An	Arch of Triumph 4
American Patrol	Flag 79
Anchors Aweigh	Anchor 2, hat, sailor 95, scales 141, stripes 162
Anniversary Song	Cake 28, wedding rings 194
Anniversary Waltz	Cake 28, wedding rings 194
Apple Blossom Time	Tree, shade 183
April in Paris	Arch of Triumph 4, Eiffel Tower 71

April in Portugal	Fan, Spanish 76, sombrero 153
April Showers	Birdbath 17
Around the World in 80 Days	Balloon 7, blimp 20, globe 88
Asleep in the Deep	Submarine 163
As Time Goes By	Clock 50
A Tisket, A Tasket	Basketball and hoop 13, Guillotine 91
Autumn Leaves	Leaf 104, tree, shade 183
Autumn Serenade	Tree, shade 183
Ave Maria	Spanish mission 154
Babes in Toyland	Carriage, baby 40, diaper 61
Baby Elephant Walk	Noah's Ark 115, tent, circus 172
Baby Face	Carriage, baby 40, cradle 56, diaper 61
Baby Love	Carriage, baby 40
Back in Your Own Back Yard	Croquet set 57, diving board 64, lawn mower 103, swing 165
Bali Hai	Tree, palm 182
Ballad of the Green Berets, The	Soldier 152
Ballet Parisien	Arch of Triumph 4, Eiffel Tower 71
Band Played On, The	Bicycle, 1890's 16
Bang Bang	Cannon 35
Barcarolle	Gondola 90
Barnum and Bailey's Favorite	Tent, circus 172
Battle Hymn of the Republic	Flag 79
Beat Goes On, The	Drum 69, metronome 112

Bells Are Ringing	Bell 14, telephone 170, wedding rings 194
Bells of St. Mary's, The	Bell 14
Best of Everything, The	Number one 117
Bewitched	Pumpkin 131, snake 149
Beyond the Blue Horizon	Balloon 7
Big Bad John	Pick 127, scales 141, wheelbarrow 195
Big Cage, The	Tent, circus 172
Bill Bailey, Won't You Please Come Home	Rolling pin 139
Black Magic Woman	Pumpkin 131, spear 155
Blowin' in the Wind	Snake and basket 150
Blow the Man Down	Anchor 2
Blueberry Hill	Ant 3
Bluebird of Happiness	Birdbath 17
Blue Champagne	Glass, wine 87
Blue Monday	Face, sad 75
Blue Skies	Barometer 12, blimp 20, sun 164
Boola Boola	Pennant 123
Boots and Saddles	Boot 22
Born Free	Balloons, carnival 8, parachute 120, sailboat 140
Boulevard of Broken Dreams, The	Parking meter 121
Brazil	Coffee pot 52
Breeze and I, The	Kite 102, wind chimes 198, windmill 199
Bridge Over the River Kwai	Bridge 26
British Grenadiers, The	Cannon 35, Gibraltar 84
Buckle Down, Winsocki	Goalpost 89
Bugle Call Rag	Cornet-trumpet 55

Bugler's Holiday	Bugler 27, cornet-trumpet 55
Bushel and a Peck, A	Chicken or turkey 44
Bus Stop	Sign, traffic 145
But the Melody Lingers On	Clef, bass 48
By the Beautiful Sea	Anchor 2, birds, gulls 19, umbrella, beach 186
Caisson Song	Cannon 35, soldier 152, stripes 162
Calcutta	Snake and basket 150
California, Here I Come	Camper 32, wagon, covered 190
Call Me Irresponsible	Telephone 170
Canadian Sunset	Sun 164
Candy	Lollipop 107
Candy and Cake	Cake 28
Candy Kisses	Booth, carnival 23, lollipop 107, scales 141
Candy Man, The	Lollipop 107
Caravan	Pyramids 132
Carnival of Venice (theme)	Gondola 90
Carousel	Ferris wheel 77
Casey Jones	Train 180
Cast Your Fate to the Wind	Crystal ball 60, sailboat 140
Catch a Falling Star	Comet 53, star 158
Cathy's Clown	Balloons, carnival 8
Chattanooga Choo-Choo	Train 180
Cherokee	Bow and Arrow 25, tomahawk 177, wigwam 197
Cherry Pink and Apple Blossom White	Leaf 104
Chevy Song	Car 38

Chicago	Skyline 146
Chicken Reel	Chicken or turkey 44, P.A. system 122
Chinatown, My Chinatown	Pagoda 119, rickshaw 135
Chopsticks	Piano 126, rickshaw 135
Climb Every Mountain	Ant 3, Bicycle, 1890's 16, mountains 114, pick 127, stairs 157
Close to You	Camera, T.V. 31, shortwave radio 144
Cocktails for Two	Bottle, chemistry 24, glass 86
Cold, Cold Heart	Igloo 101, snowman 151
Come Rain or Come Shine	Umbrella table 188
Cool, Cool Water	Glass 86, pyramids 132
Coronation March	Crown 59
Cotton Candy	Tightrope 176
Count Every Star	Metronome 112
Cross Over the Bridge	Bridge 26
Cruising Down the River	Fishing pole 78, gondola 90, river boat 138, ship 143
Crusader's Hymn	Church 45
Cry Me a River	Bridge 26, face, sad 75, river boat 138
Cuddle Up a Little Closer	Cat 43
Dance of the Paper Dolls	Doll house 67
Dancing in the Dark	Candelabra 33, candle 34, P.A. system 122
Days of Wine and Roses	Calendar 29, glass, wine 87, table 167
Day the Rains Came, The	Noah's Ark 115, rainbow 134, umbrella, rain 187
Dear John Letter, A	Envelope 72
Deep River	Submarine 163

Desert Song	Camel 30, pyramids 132, tank 168
Dig You Later	Ant 3, pick 127
Dinner at Eight	Candelabra 33, candle 34, coffee pot 52, table 167
Dixie	Cap, Confederate 36
Doin' What Comes Natur'lly	Sharp-flat-natural signs 142
Doll Dance, The	Doll house 67
Don't Fence Me in	Chicken or turkey 44, padlock 118
Don't Let the Rain Come Down	Noah's Ark 115, rainbow 134
Don't Sit Under the Apple Tree	Tree, shade 183
Do-Re-Mi	Notes 116
Down in the Valley	Hat, cowboy 94
Downtown	Hat, sailor 95, skyline 146, water tower 193
Down Yonder	Carriage 39
Dragnet	Badge 6, whistle 196
Dream	Sleep sounds 148, wishing well 200
Drifting and Dreaming	Anchor 2, gondola 90, parachute 120, sleep sounds 148
Drinking Song	Birdbath 17, coffee pot 52, glass 86, water tower 193
Drink to Me Only with Thine Eyes	Glass, wine 87, water tower 193
Drums in My Heart	Drum 69
Dry Bones	Water tower 193
Dum Dum	Cap, dunce 37
East of the Sun	Compass 54

Ebb Tide	Anchor 2, birds, gulls 19, hat, sailor 95, river boat 138, ship 143
Entry of the Gladiators	Tent, circus 172
Falling in Love with Love	Bow and arrow 25, parachute 120, teetertotter 169
Far Away Places	Shortwave radio 144
Farmer in the Dell, The	Barn 10, barn and silo 11, chicken or turkey 44, pitchfork 130, tractor 179
Feudin' and Fightin'	Rifle 136, stripes 162, tank 168
Fire	Pipe 129
Five Foot Two	Thermometer 174
Five Minutes More	Dice 62, hangman's noose 92, parking meter 121
Flamingo	Birdhouse 18, Noah's Ark 115
Flat Foot Floogee, The	Sharp-flat-natural signs 142
Foggy Day, A	Skyline 146
Folsom Prison Blues	Padlock 118
Fools Rush In	Cap, dunce 37
Four Walls, The	Castle 42, dice 62
From Rags to Riches	Dollar sign 66
Frosty the Snowman	Snowman 151
Game of Love	Pinball Machine 128
Games People Play	Croquet set 57, pinball machine 128, tic-tac-toe 175
Gaudemus Igitur	Pennant 123
Georgy Girl	Girl 85
Get Together	Megaphone 111

Ghost Riders in the Sky	Horse 97
Gillette Look Sharp March	Goalpost 89, sharp-flat-natural signs 142
Girl of My Dreams	Girl 85
Girl That I Marry, The	Girl 85, ring or wheel 137
God Bless America	Church 45, flag 79, Washington Monument 192
God Save the Queen	Crown 59
Goin' Out of My Head	Guillotine 91, sign, traffic 145
Golden Earrings	Pick 127
Goldfinger	Cash register 41
Gone Fishin'	Fishing pole 78
Grandfather's Clock	Clock 50
Green Fields	Barn and silo 11
Green, Green	Cash register 41, lawn mower 103
Green Green Grass of Home	Barn and silo 11, croquet set, 57, lawn mower 103, leaf 104, light, traffic 106
Gunsmoke	Rifle 136
Halls of Ivy	Mortarboard 113, pennant 123
Hanging Tree, The	Hangman's noose 92
Happy Birthday to You	Cake 28
Happy Wanderer, The	Ant 3, camel 30, face, happy 74
Harper Valley P.T.A.	Lectern 105
Harp That Once, Thro' Tara's Halls, The	Harp 93
Hawaiian War Chant	Drum 69, tree, palm 182
Hawaiian Wedding Song	Tree, palm 182
Hawaii Five-O	Badge 6, tree, palm 182

Heart	Four-H 82
Heartaches	Four-H 82, heart 96, hypodermic needle 100, machine gun 108, stairs 157
Heart of My Heart	Heart 96
Heat Wave	Pitchfork 130, sun 164
Hello, Dolly!	Walkie-talkies 191
Here's to Romance	Glass, wine 87
Hernando's Hideway	Badge 6
He's Got the Whole World in His Hands	Cross 58, Four-H 82
Hey, Look Me Over	Camera, T.V. 31, periscope 124, snake 149, telescope 171
Hey There	Megaphone 111
Hickory, Dickory Dock	Clock 50
High and the Mighty, The	Airplane 1, balloon 7, bicycle, 1890's 16, mountains 114
High Hopes	Barbell 9, bicycle, 1890's 16, blimp 20, diving board 64, mountains 114, Noah's Ark 115
High Noon	Hat, cowboy 94
High Society	Ant 3
Holiday for Strings	Harp 93
Holiday for Trombones	Trombone 184
Holy, Holy, Holy	Cross 58
Home on the Range	Hat, cowboy 94
Home Sweet Home	Camper 32, castle 42, house 99
Hoop-dee-doo	Croquet set 57
Hot Canary	Birdhouse 18
Hot Diggity	Pitchfork 130

Hot Lips	Cigarette pack 47
Hot Time in the Old Town, A	Pitchfork 130
House of the Rising Sun	House 99, pagoda 119, rickshaw 135, turtle 185
How Deep Is the Ocean	Submarine 163
How Do You Speak to an Angel?	Question mark 133, walkie-talkies 191
How Dry I Am	Camel 30, carriage, baby 40
How Great Thou Art	Dinosaur 63, scales 141
How the West Was Won	Compass 54, rifle 136, wagon, covered 190
I Ain't Got Nobody	Face, sad 75, Guillotine 91
I Almost Lost My Mind	Guillotine 91
I Could Have Danced All Night	P.A. System 122
I Cover the Waterfront	Diving board 64, machine gun 108
I'd Like to Teach the World to Sing	Lectern 105
I Don't Want to Set the World on Fire	Match 110
I Feel Fine	Four-H 82
I Feel Good	Four-H 82
If I Knew You Were Comin, I'd 'ave Baked a Cake	Cake 28
I Get a Kick Out of You	Cannon 35, goalpost 89, rifle 136
I Got Rhythm	Drum 69, metronome 112
I Hear a Rhapsody	Clef, bass 48, clef, treble 49, phonograph 125, short-wave radio 144, wind chimes 198
I Kiss Your Hand, Madame	Booth, carnival 23

I'll Be Seeing You	Periscope 124, telescope 171
I'll Never Smile Again	Hypodermic needle 100
I'll String Along with You	Hangman's Noose 92, harp 93, kite 102
I'll Walk Alone	Number One 117, tightrope 176
I'll Walk the Line	Tightrope 176
I Love Paris	Arch of Triumph 4, Eiffel tower 71, fountain 81
I'm Always Chasing Rainbows	Piano 126, rainbow 134
I'm an Old Cowhand	Boot 22, horse 97
I'm Headin' for the Last Roundup	Horse 97
I'm Looking Over a Four Leaf Clover	Four leaf clover 83
Impossible Dream, The	Sleep sounds 148, Spanish mission 154
I'm Shooting High	Airplane 1, rifle 136
I'm Sitting on Top of the World	Globe 88, kite 102, mountains 114, teeter-totter 169
In a Little Spanish Town	Fan, Spanish 76, sombrero 153
In An Eighteenth Century Drawing Room	Drawing board 68
In an Old Dutch Garden	Windmill 199
Indian Love Call	Bow and arrow 25, snake and basket 150, tomahawk 177, wigwam 197
Indian Reservation	Tomahawk 177
Indian Summer	Bow and arrow 25, wigwam 197
In My Merry Oldsmobile	Car 38
In the Good Old Summer Time	Diving board 64, fishing pole 78, tractor 179

I Only Have Eyes for You	Periscope 124
I See Your Face Before Me	·Crystal ball 60, periscope 124
It Is No Secret	Padlock 118
It's a Good Day	Calendar 29
It's All in the Game	Croquet set 57, pinball machine 128, tic-tac-toe 175
It's Later Than You Think	Bomb 21
It's So Nice to Have a Man Around the House	Lawn mower 103
It Was a Very Good Year	Blimp 20, calendar 29
I've Been Working on the Railroad	Ant 3, pick 127, wheelbarrow 195
I've Got You Under My Skin	Hypodermic needle 100
Ivory Tower	Pennant 123
I Want a Girl	Girl 85
I Whistle a Happy Tune	Clef, bass 48
I Will Wait for You	Parking meter 121, sign, traffic 145
I Wish I Didn't Love You So	Wishing well 200
I Wish You Love	Wishing well 200
Jailhouse Rock	Padlock 118
Japanese Sandman	Rickshaw 135
Java	Coffee pot 52
Jersey Bounce	Basketball and hoop 13
Josephine	Girl 85
Jumpin' at the Woodside	Parachute 120
Keep It a Secret	Padlock 118
Kewpie Doll	Doll house 67
King of the Road	Camper 32, car 38, carriage 39, cigarette pack 47, crown 59

Kiss of Fire	Booth, carnival 23
Lady of Spain	Fan, Spanish 76, sombrero 153
La Marsellaise	Arch of Triumph 4
Lamp Is Low, The	Street light 160
Lamplighter's Serenade	Street light 160
Laura	Girl 85
Lazy Bones	Fishing pole 78, sleep sounds 148
Let It Snow! Let It Snow! Let It Snow!	Sled 147, snowman 151
Let Me Call You Sweetheart	Telephone 170
Let's Have Another Cup of Coffee	Table 167
Liberty Bell March	Victory (peace) sign 189
Light My Fire	Candle 34, cigarette lighter 46, cigarette pack 47, match 110, pipe 129
Lion Sleeps Tonight, The	Cat 43
Listen to the Mockingbird	Birdbath 17, birdhouse 18
Little Brown Church, The	Church 45
Little Drummer Boy	Drum 69
Little Green Apples	Leaf 104
Little Things Mean a Lot	Scales 141
London Bridge is Falling Down	Bridge 26
Lonely Bull, The	Fan, Spanish 76, sombrero 153
Look for the Silver Lining	Crystal ball 60, skyline 146, tote bag 178
Look of Love	Telescope 171
Love and Marriage	Ring or wheel 137
Love for Sale	Cash register 41

Love Is a Many-Splendored Thing	Fountain 81, harp 93
Love Is Blue	Easel, canvas 70
Love Letters in the Sand	Envelope 72, mailbox 109
Lucky in Love	Four leaf clover 83
Lullaby of Broadway	Stage 156, street sign 161
Mack the Knife	Sword 166
Magnificent Seven, The	Hat, cowboy 94
Make Believe	Balloons, carnival 8, camera, T.V. 31, doll house 67, pumpkin 131, stage 156, tote bag 178
Mama Inez	Rolling pin 139
Mam'selle	Eiffel Tower 71
Manhattan Serenade	Skyline 146
Man with a Horn	Bugler 27, cornet-trumpet 55
March from Aida	Arch of Triumph 4
Marching Through Georgia	Cap, Confederate 36
March of the Little Leaden Soldiers	Soldier 152, whistle 196
Marine's Hymn	Machine gun 108, soldier 152, stripes 162
Meet Me in St. Louis, Louis	Balloons, carnival 8, Ferris wheel 77
Memories Are Made of This	Carriage 39
Merry-Go-Round Broke Down, The	Balloons, carnival 8
Mississippi Mud	Cap, Confederate 36
Misty	Skyline 146
Mona Lisa	Easel, canvas 70
Moonglow	Telescope 171

Mr. Lucky	Four leaf clover 83, pinball machine 128
Mr. Sandman	Camel 30
Mule Train	Wagon, covered 190
Music! Music! Music!	Clef, treble 49, notes 116, phonograph 125, stereo, cassette 159
Music to Watch Girls By	Clef, treble 49, girl 85, notes 116, stereo-cassette 159
My Coloring Book	Easel, canvas 70
My Heart Cries for You	Heart 96, hypodermic needle 100
My Heart Tells Me	Cigarette pack 47, scales 141
My Old Flame	Candle 34, match 110
Nature Boy	Dinosaur 63
Naughty Lady of Shady Lane	Tree, shade 183
New World Symphony Themes	Globe 88
Night and Day	Street light 160
Night Train	Train 180
Nobody knows de Trouble I've Seen	Face, sad 75
North to Alaska	Camper 32, compass 54, igloo 101
Now Is the Hour	Clock 50, hourglass 98
Oh, Happy Day	Face, happy 74
Oh What a Beautiful Morning	Barn 10
Old Devil Moon	Pitchfork 130
Old Grey Mare, The	Barn 10, carriage 39
Old MacDonald Had a Farm	Barn and silo 11, tractor 179
Old Rugged Cross, The	Cross 58
Ol' Man River	River boat 138

On a Bicycle Built for Two	Bicycle 15
On a Clear Day You Can See Forever	Birds, gulls 19
On a Slow Boat to China	Rickshaw 135
Once in Love with Amy	Number One 117
One Alone	Number One 117
One Dozen Roses	Flower 80, thermometer 174
One O'Clock Jump	Dice 62, diving board 64
One Who Really Loves You	Number One 117
One World	Globe 88
On the Good Ship Lollipop	Lollipop 107, tree, palm 182
On the Street Where You Live	Castle 42, house 99, street sign 161
On the Trail	Spear 155, wagon, covered 190
On Top of Old Smoky	Pipe 129
Onward Christian Soldiers	Cross 58
On Wisconsin	Megaphone 111
Over and Over	Goalpost 89
Over the Rainbow	Rainbow 134
Over the Waves	Ship 143, shortwave radio 144
PA 6500	Telephone 170
Paint It Black	Easel, canvas 70
Paint Your Wagon	Easel, canvas 70
Parade of the Wooden Soldiers	Soldier 152
Peaceful Valley	Victory (peace) sign 189
Peanut Vendor, The	Tightrope 176
Pennies From Heaven	Cash register 41, dollar sign 66, parking meter 121
Penny Lane	Cash register 41

Peter Gunn	Machine gun 108, rifle 136, shortwave radio 144
Picnic	Ant 3, umbrella table 188
Pictures from an Exposition	Camera, T.V. 31, easel, canvas 70
Pink Panther	Cat 43, spear 155, tent, circus 172
Play a Simple Melody	Clef, bass 48, stereo, cassette 159
Please Mr. Postman	Envelope 72, mailbox 109
Poor People of Paris, The	Dollar sign 66, Eiffel Tower 71
Prisoner of Love	Badge 6, castle 42, padlock 118
P.S. I Love You	Heart 96, mailbox 109
Puff	Cigarette lighter 46
Put on a Happy Face	Face, happy 74, pumpkin 131, tote bag 178
Put Your Arms Around Me, Honey	Goalpost 89
Rachmaninoff's Concerto	Piano 126
Rain	Cloud, rain 51
Raindrops	Umbrella, rain 187
Raindrops Keep Falling on My Head	Barometer 12, cloud, rain 51 umbrella, rain 187
Rain in Spain, The	Umbrella, rain 187
Ramblin' Wreck from Georgia Tech	Drawing board 68
Red River Valley	Hat, cowboy 94
Red Roses For a Blue Lady	Flower 80, light, traffic 106
Red Sails in the Sunset	Sailboat 140, ship 143
Red Wing	Birdhouse 18
Reflections	Tote bag 178

Rhapsody in Blue	Notes 116, piano 126
Rhythm of the Rain	Fountain 81, metronome 112
Right as the Rain	Cloud, rain 51
Ritual Fire Dance	Cigarette lighter 46, pipe 129, pitchfork 130
Rock-A-Bye Baby	Cradle 56, diaper 61
Rock and Roll Waltz	Gibraltar 84
Rock Around the Clock	Gibraltar 84
Rock of Ages	Gibraltar 84
Roses Are Red	Flower 80
Round and Round	Bicycle 15, Ferris wheel 77, machine gun 108, phonograph 125, ring or wheel 137
Route 66	Camper 32, thermometer 174
Row, Row, Row Your Boat	Hat, sailor 95
Rule, Brittania	Gibraltar 84
Rum and Coca-Cola	Glass 86
Sabre Dance	Sword 166
Sail Along, Silvery Moon	Sailboat 140
Say It with Music	Notes 116
Scarborough Fair—Canticle	Booth, carnival 23
School Days, School Days	Cap, dunce 37, lectern 105, mortarboard 113, teeter-totter 169, tic-tac-toe 175
See You Later, Alligator	Tent, circus 172
Send for Me	Envelope 72, mailbox 109
Seventy-Six Trombones	Thermometer 174, trombone 184
Shadow of Your Smile, The	Candle 34, face, happy 74
Shake, Rattle and Roll	Snake 149

Sheik of Araby, The	Pyramids 132
She Wore a Yellow Ribbon	Light, traffic 106
Shoe Shine Boy	Boot 22
Shrimp Boats	Hat, sailor 95
Side by Side	Walkie-talkies 191
Sidewalks of New York, The	Bicycle 15
Sincerely	Envelope 72, mailbox 109
Sing For Your Supper	Table 167
Singin' in the Rain	Clef, bass 48, cloud, rain 51, umbrella, rain 187
Sink the Bismark	Submarine 163
Sitting By the Window	Coffee pot 52
Sixteen Tons	Pick 127, scales 141, turtle 185, wheelbarrow 195
Slaughter on Tenth Avenue	Street sign 161
Sleep	Sleep sounds 148
Sleepy Lagoon, A	Birds, gulls 19
Sleepy Time Gal	Sleep sounds 148
Sleigh Ride	Sled 147
Slipping Around	Sled 147, trombone 184
Slowpoke	Cap, dunce 37, sign, traffic 145, turtle 185
Smilin' Through	Face, happy 74
Smoke Gets in Your Eyes	Candelabra 33, cigarette lighter 46, cigarette pack 47, match 110, pipe 129, skyline 146
Snow Bird	Igloo 101, snowman 151
So Far Away	Shortwave radio 144
Some Day My Prince Will Come	Castle 42, crown 59
Something's Gotta Give	Machine gun 108
Song of India	Snake 149, snake and basket 150

Those Were The Days	Calendar 29, carriage 39
Three Bells, The	Bell 14, Spanish mission 154
Three Coins in the Fountain	Dice 62, fountain 81
Tiger Rag	Cat 43, spear 155, tent, circus 172
Till the End of Time	Clock 50, hangman's noose 92, hourglass 98
Time on My Hands	Hourglass 98, metronome 112
Tiptoe, Through the Tulips	Flower 80
Together	Megaphone 111
Too Fat Polka	Barbell 9, scales 141
Too-ra-loo-ra-loo-ral	Four leaf clover 83
To Sir with Love	Envelope 72
Trail of the Lonesome Pine The	Tree, Christmas or pine 181
Travelin' Man	Car 38
Tree in the Meadow, The	Leaf 104, tree, Christmas or pine 181
Trees	Tree, Christmas or pine 181
Trumpeter's Lullaby	Bugler 27, cornet-trumpet 55
Tumbling Tumbleweeds	Hat, cowboy 94
Turkey in the Straw	Chicken or turkey 44, P.A. system 122
Turn! Turn! Turn!	Arrow 5, parking meter 121
Twist, The	Parking meter 121
Two Cigarettes in the Dark	Cigarette lighter 46, cigarette pack 47, match 110
2001 Space Odyssey	Bottle, chemistry 24
Undecided	Teeter-totter 169
Under a Blanket of Blue	Tent, pup 173

Up Tight	Stairs 157
Up, Up and Away	Balloon 7, barbell 9, basketball and hoop 13, blimp 20, kite 102, stairs 157, teeter-totter 169
Vaya Con Dios	Spanish mission 154
Victor's March	Victory (peace) sign 189
Victory at Sea	Hat, sailor 95, ship 143, submarine 163, victory (peace) sign 189
Wagon Wheels	Wagon, covered 190
Waiting for the Robert E. Lee	River boat 138
Wait 'Til the Sun Shines Nellie	Sign, traffic 145
Wake the Town and Tell the People	Bell 14, church 45
Wake Up and Live	Hourglass 98
Walk, Don't Run	Arrow 5, hangman's noose 92, light, traffic 106
Walkin' My Baby Back Home	Carriage, baby 40, dog 65
Walk on By	Arrow 5, boot 22, dinosaur 63, snake 149
Walk Right In	Arrow 5
Warsaw Concerto	Piano 126
Washington and Lee Swing	Washington Monument 192
Washington Post March	Washington Monument 192
Waterloo	Water tower 193
Wedding March	Church 45, ring or wheel 137, wedding rings 194
We're in the Money	Cash register 41, dollar sign 66
Whatever Lola Wants	Question mark 133, rolling pin 139

Whatever Will Be, Will Be	Crystal ball 60
What Kind of Fool Am I?	Cap, dunce 37
What Now My Love	Question mark 133
What the World Needs Now Is Love	Globe 88
Wheel of Fortune	Bicycle, 1890's 16, ring or wheel 137
When It's Sleepy Time Down South	Sleep sounds 148
When My Baby Smiles at Me	Cradle 56, diaper 61
When You're Hot, You're Hot	Sun 164
When You Wish Upon a Star	Comet 53, star 158, wishing well 200
Where, O Where Has My Little Dog Gone?	Dog 65
Where the Boys Are	Arrow 5, sailboat 140, umbrella, beach 186
Whiffenpoof Song, The	Mortarboard 113, pennant 123
Whistle While You Work	Wheelbarrow 195, whistle 196
Who?	Question mark 133
Why Don't You Believe Me	Badge 6, question mark 133
Wichita Lineman	Drawing board 68, telephone 170
Winchester Cathedral	Bell 14, church 45, megaphone 111
Windmills of Your Mind	Windmill 199
Windy	Barometer 12, kite 102, sailboat 140, ship 143, wind chimes 198, windmill 199
Wine, Woman and Song	Glass, wine 87
Winter Wonderland	Igloo 101, snowman 151

Wipe Out	Car 38
Wish You Were Here	Wishing well 200
World Without Love, A	Globe 88
Yankee Doodle	Washington Monument 192
Yellow Bird	Birdhouse 18, light, traffic 106
Yes Sir, That's My Baby	Cradle 56, doll house 67, rolling pin 139
Yesterday	Calendar 29
You Ain't Nothin' But a Hound Dog	Dog 65
You Always Hurt the One You Love	Hypodermic needle 100, rolling pin 139, spear 155, sword 166
You Are My Lucky Star	Star 158
You Go to My Head	Ferris wheel 77, four-H 82, Guillotine 91, rolling pin 139, tomahawk 177
Your Cheatin' Heart	Heart 96, tic-tac-toe 175
You're in the Army Now	Tent, pup 173
You're Sensational	Cap, dunce 37
You're the Top	Number One 117
You Turned the Tables on Me	Table 167
Zing! Went the Strings of My Heart	Bow and arrow 25, harp 93